BETWEEN
HIS
SHOULDERS

By
Barbara Ann Chase

Prepared by Companion Press for:

ACCORD COMPANY
P.O. Box 326
Kingsland, TX 78639

ISBN 1-56043-470-8

For Worldwide Distribution
Printed in the U.S.A.

BETWEEN HIS SHOULDERS

*OF BENJAMIN HE SAID, "MAY THE
BELOVED OF THE LORD DWELL IN SECURITY BY
HIM, WHO SHIELDS HIM
ALL THE DAY, AND HE DWELLS
BETWEEN HIS SHOULDERS"*

Deuteronomy 33:12 (NAS)

MAY YOU READ THIS BOOK
WITH CHILDLIKE FAITH
LOOKING FOR GOOD.

DEDICATED TO

GOD'S BELOVED SON WITH WHOM HE
IS WELL PLEASED, OUR BROTHER
JESUS.

Table of Contents

Part One: Safely Home

The StoryTeller 3

The Chipmunk Story 4

The Beautiful Gate 7

Send Me O God 11

Faith in His Children 12

Sons from Afar 16

Part Two: Shepherd's Call

Come! 19

More 21

More than Green Meadows 22

Sheltered 25

Moving 27

Picture Frames 28

Sequence 30

Part Three: Saints and Sin

Why Saints Sin 35

Mary in the Kitchen 37

An Attentive Son 40

God, The Holy Spirit 44

Descending Love 47

Beloved Children 48

I've Cried Before 51

Part Four: Starry Nights

Dear Jesus 55

All by Starlight 56

Gideon, by Cover of Night 60

The Night of Betrayal 63

Separation 64

Choices in the Night 65

Part Five: Seasons' Bloom

Roses 69

The Beholder 70

Delphinium 72

Fire and Flowers 73

God's Seasons 74

I Adore You! 77

Part Six: Stillness

Solitude 81

Brownbag 83

In So Many Ways, Unspoken 84

God's Voice 85

Almost 90

Loyalty 91

Part Seven: Stonework

Rocks 95

Our God The Rock 100

A Rock Formation 102

Awareness 103

God's Friends 106

Father 108

Not Forsaken 109

Part Eight: Sons Who Serve

Mistaken Identity 113

For Al on his Birthday 114

Sparklers (for Katie) 115

Two Sons 117

To Build a House

(dedicated to Bobby Roark) 125

One Widow's Might 126

Part Nine: Summits

To be a Friend 131

A Neighbor 132

Just Cause 135

Jerusalem at a Distance 138

Twice Anointed 139

Beautiful on the Mountain 140

ACKNOWLEDGEMENTS

In this my first book I would like to acknowledge those who have given me some of my literary "firsts".

Mom—my first exposure to God's word in the big family bible.

Dad—my first view of history through his stamp catalogues.

My sisters and brothers—my first membership in a community of readers.

Sister Mary Joseph, sixth grade teacher—my first and best instruction in English grammar.

Sister Ingrid Doyle, journalism teacher—my first awareness of the power of words.

Sister Theophane—my first taste for philosophical journals.

Rollie Danielson—my first prodder. "How is your book coming?"

Joe and Rutheann Aldridge—my first bound-manuscript producers.

Babe and Mildred Fryar—my first check designated "book publication".

Companion Press—my first experience with a ministry that will bless, break and multiply the word of God for distribution.

I am grateful to these as well as Gordon and Emily Binning, my Valley of Praise family, my board of directors—Bobby Roark, Bob and Carol Steinruck—and other dear and faithful friends whose names are recorded in the Lamb's book of life.

ABOUT THE AUTHOR

Perhaps you've met Barbara Ann Chase... at a Valley of Praise Ministry location or been taught by her when she was on the Women's Aglow Fellowship International Board. Or maybe you celebrated with her at a Feast of Tabernacles in Jerusalem when she was a representative of the International Christian Embassy.

Could Barbara Ann have ministered in prophecy to you at one of her Together Ministries Retreats or helped change your life when she was overseeing the Corpus Christi Institute in Texas?

Barbara Ann Chase has touched the lives of thousands during twenty years of ministry in over twenty countries. Are you one who received a word of encouragement in a Renewal meeting in Scotland, a Greek restaurant in Alaska, or a farmhouse in Sweden? She may have shared with you on a jungle train in Costa Rica or riding a crowded matatu in Kenya.

Barbara Ann is used by God to help you hear Jesus and tell you simple beautiful stories of His great saving love.

by Linda Shore

FOREWORD

Words are like colored oils upon an artist's brush. When applied to the canvas of our minds, they paint vivid pictures filled with feeling, meaning and motivation. With the skill of a divinely gifted artist, Barbara Ann Chase has graced the family of God with a gallery of inspired scenes which are brilliant in beauty and fresh in their composition. Each scene is a story in which the character and purposes of God are revealed in an intimate and personal way.

"Between His Shoulders" is a most picturesque phrase. We see a weak, wounded and frightened little lamb brought into a positional relationship of rest, peace, strength and safety. But it is much more than that. Moses' blessing upon Benjamin pictured a future day in which God would draw His people by His Spirit into personal fellowship with Himself—and each other. Similar figures of speech would include, "upon His heart" or "within His embrace." In a word, the concept is companionship!

This theme of God's love for His people—a Father's love for His family—is woven through each of the stories and poems in this delightful volume in such a winsome way that the reader is inspired to worship. It is a quality of worship, however, that seeks to bring the Lord glory, honor, power and pleasure through a life of childlike trust and obedience.

As might be expected, the strength of each story is to be found in the spiritual life of the storyteller. Barbara Ann is sharing with us divine insights which she has gathered over many years and from many places in her personal walk with God. Each truth has been drawn from experience and is worthy of our time and reflection.

"Between His Shoulders" is a superb devotional book because of the size and content of each chapter. It is also a goldmine of spiritual truth that can enrich your life in the Lord in very personal and practical ways. I am sure you will find, as did I, that your desire will become divided between lingering with the thoughts of each story, and moving quickly on to the next with a sense of fresh anticipation. Either way, read it with expectation; you will not be disappointed!

Dr. Robert Frost

INTRODUCTION

Now this is the blessing with which Moses
the man of God blessed the sons of Israel
before his death.
Of Benjamin [son of my right hand] he said,
"May the Beloved of the Lord dwell in
security by him who shields him all the day,
and he dwells between his shoulders."

Deuteronomy 33:12 (NAS)

Between His Shoulders is a description of Benjamin's inheritance as proclaimed in the blessing of Moses before his death. As a book title it ties together essays and poem studies that span a twenty year period. While much of this book deals with God's children, its heart is to reveal the Father's Love. There can be no love without reverence. Jesus says, "If you love me you will keep my commandments."

I can think of few moments in the Old Testament as heartbreaking as those solemn moments when Ezekiel saw in vision, God's Glory departing from His temple. His Glory filled the inner court as the cherubim stood on the right side of the temple. A man clothed in white linen filled his hands with coals to scatter over the city. Then the Glory went up to the threshold of the temple and the court was filled with the brightness of that Glory. The wings of the cherubim were heard in the outer court. The cherubim and the whirling wheels from between them with the spirit of the living beings in them, rose and stood still at the East Gate of the Lord's house. And the Glory of God hovered over them. There were twenty-five evil advisers at the entrance of the East Gate. There was a much-loved people that God would judge because they acted like the nations around them and feared men rather than God.

Ezekiel cried out for a remnant and the Lord comforted him. As the Glory of God hovered over the city and then stood over the mountain east of the city, Ezekiel had God's word. God promised to scatter and then to gather a people who would remove all detestable things. He would give them a new heart and spirit. He would give them the land of Israel. He would be their God and they would be His people. God waits for His sons. When He withdraws, it is with reluctance. He lingers at each stage of His departure. Even His withdrawing is to draw us. How close would God have us? Like Benjamin, He would have us dwell Between His Shoulders.

From that vantage point, secure within His government and next to His heart, we would anticipate His way. If He wanted to heal a woodland creature or reveal His wisdom to little children that would be one more reason to worship Him. Between His Shoulders, we are at home and more at ease with our brothers Moshe (Moses) and David, Kefa (Peter) and Shaul (Paul). We find that His ways, sovereignly and through our brothers are not grievous but filled with order and beauty. Between His Shoulders we see the solution to Martha's anxiety and we see hope for the prodigal. The Good Samaritan is there with Brother Lawrence. Between His Shoulders the darkest night is as light and the shadows of Gethsemane are folded up with the grave cloths. The parables are explained and bread broken. From Between His Shoulders, fathers return to their children and children to their fathers. God is a Refuge and a Rock. Be encouraged!

Barbara Ann Chase
January 1991

PART ONE

SAFELY HOME

"For God sent not His Son into the world to condemn the world; but that the world through Him might be saved."

John 3:17

THE STORYTELLER

The stories were told
long before papyrus
yielded to the markings
of primitive man.

Where did the stories come from?
Where did they go?
Children used to know.

Since libraries sealed up history
by volume and Bibles
were chained to the floor,
like lost illuminations
Children have ceased to know

That their fathers walked
with God, the Storyteller
living letters in a Book
open to all,
First edition, never out of print
History revealed in Bethlehem
to children baking bread.

THE CHIPMUNK STORY

"Please tell the chipmunk story again." I hear this request frequently as I return to the places I have spoken. In the Netherlands and Germany where to my knowledge there are no chipmunks, the children ask about the little creature, or the sick squirrel.

I have wondered how an illustration becomes a story. I think that it is a combination of universal appeal on the inside and appreciation on the outside. In the case of the chipmunk story, the appeal and appreciation are similar to those elicited by Jesus when He assures us in Matthew 6:26 of our infinite worth. He says, "look at the birds of the air (study them deeply). They do not sow nor reap nor store away in barns and yet your heavenly Father feeds them. Are you not much more valuable than they?"

Gordon and Emily are my friends. They live in an elegant log home, octagonal in shape and warm in spirit. They built the home themselves in a secluded corner of Eastern Idaho. This home, primitive only in the absence of telephone and television, has been my hideaway and first aid station for many years.

One day as one of my visits with Gordon and Emily was drawing to a close, the chipmunk came. He came hobbling along the fence rail trying to keep his balance. Then amazingly he was on the window ledge pressing his face and paws against the kitchen window. Emily and I paused in our dishwashing. It is not usual for a wild chipmunk to come so near. They aren't like the tame city squirrels whom I suspect of pounding front doors and demanding food.

As we looked, we saw that this scraggly-tailed chipmunk either had been injured or was diseased. Extending the length of his body was a very large tumor or growth and in the growth three dark black holes. Was it our imagination or had God sent this little one to us that, in a small way, we might comfort creation? Emily and I lifted our hands toward the chipmunk and prayed for its healing before it slipped away along the fence rail and into the meadow.

The next day, I returned home and several days later received a letter from Emily. It was filled with exclamation points; this was not unusual. Emily is one of those exclamation point people who truly enjoy the journey to heaven. But her exclamations disclosed a second encounter. The day after I left, Emily was standing at the sink when a chipmunk scampered along the fence rail, jumped onto the window ledge, and pressed its face and paws against the window. The growth was gone. Could it possibly have been another chipmunk? God knows how we talk ourselves out of miracles. And perhaps for that reason, when Emily drew closer, she saw three tiny scars where the holes had been. The chipmunk had come back to say "thank you" and to remind us of our worth.

The scraggly tail? Months after his fur had covered over the scars, his tail identified him as one whose frequent visits qualified him as a homebody.

***

God's creatures can know when our intentions toward them are good and someday, when we are in need, if we have cared for them, God may use them to lead us to safety.

ROMANS 8:19

*"For the earnest expectation of the
creature waiteth for the manifestation
of the sons of God."*

THE BEAUTIFUL GATE

When I was growing up I was fascinated by the stories of the men and women in both the Old and New Testament. The Old Testament prophets, by the Holy Spirit, could shake and shape nations; and whether it was Hannah's faith, Esther's courage, or Deborah's wisdom, women swelled the ranks of the valiant. In the New Testament, the mystery of God's love not only continued to unfold, but enfolded every man as Jesus Christ the Son of God tabernacled among us and revealed the heart of His Father. While most of the books of the Old Testament concluded with challenges, prayers and "thus saith the Lord's," and the New Testament teamed with "Amen's," the book we call Acts of Apostles ended, if not literally at least practically, with a comma.

This book of Acts led me on an adventure that is still in process today. In it, I saw ordinary men and women filled with the Holy Spirit working miracles one minute and squabbling the next. There is no record of pious airs or split personalities trying to reconcile spirit and flesh. The Incarnation seemed to be enlarged through Jesus' followers. Like the loaves and fishes, they were blessed, broken and multiplied.

I recall having read Acts, chapter three which begins with the story of the cripple healed at the Gate Beautiful. As a child, I had heard reports of healings taking place at Lourdes and had seen crutches hanging at Mother Cabrini's shrine, yet I had not seen any local miracles. We, like those of many other denominations, believed our church to be the true Church. And I remember thinking, if this is so, why is

our Church not like the church in the book of Acts. If anything, we should be resembling Jesus even more perfectly
after two thousand years. Where were the greater works He
said we would do? I asked my Protestant friends, but they
knew little more than I. Years later, when I was in the Convent and Ron McCollum, a parishioner from Dennis
Bennett's church brought me news of a personal pentecost, I
knew that Jesus had answered my question and that this
was another wave that would prepare for the time when
"the earth would be filled with the knowledge of the Lord as
the waters cover the sea" (Isaiah 11:9).

As I have continued to appreciate Acts, chapter three, I
have found in it a beautiful example of witness, particularly
when we are yearning for a balanced compassionate faith.
Salvation is an aspect of healing, a word which has within its
definition not only healing but deliverance, enlargement
and wholeness. In Acts Chapter three, we find a pattern of
administering salvation that can be of great service today.
Having first recognized as historically true the story of a real
man who was literally healed by two disciples in the name
of Jesus by the gate called Beautiful, we can safely apply elements of that story in a real way to our own lives.

The chapter begins with Peter and John going up
together into the temple at the hour of prayer, being the
ninth hour. While there are times when we are called to go to
the house of God alone, it is wise and often more enjoyable
to go with a friend. Peter and John, though newly baptized
in the Holy Spirit, did not neglect nor consider as bondage
the customary time and place of prayer. If we have desired
the privilege of introducing a person to Jesus, we will note
that it is while we are on our way to the house of the Lord
(i.e., aware of His presence) and in unity with our brothers
that this introduction is likely to happen.

Now, a certain man, lame from his mother's womb, was
carried whom they laid daily at the gate of the temple which

is called Beautiful, to ask alms of them that entered into the temple.

It speaks of God's love, that the Holy Spirit through Luke, the writer of Acts, does not refer to just any man, but a certain man—a man like all men with whom God is thoroughly familiar. This man has been lame, unable to walk, from his mother's womb. All of us come into this life crippled in one way or another, unable to walk in the way of Life, being carried along by the crowd, or those who love us, to the Gate Beautiful, but not through.

Have you ever known a person, or been one yourself, who was always at religious gatherings, unable to enter in but attempting to vicariously participate in the intimate experiences of others. They are like the lame man at the Gate saying "What is it like inside." Can we remember when we asked that question or wanted to?

The Gate Beautiful, of course, reminds us of Jesus; and it is sad to see someone sitting so close to Jesus begging alms from men. The cripple, long ago, ceased looking at the gate; but, this day, seeing Peter and John about to go into the temple, asked for alms. We often miss our opportunity to bring Salvation to people because we're in a hurry or we're distracted by where we think we should be. Peter and John stopped and gave this man their full, undivided attention. "Peter fastening his eyes upon him, with John said 'Look on us.'" To be a witness of God's love for a person, we must be willing not only to look him in the eye but to also risk saying "Look on us." Witnessing involves relationship and ongoing commitment. It begins with eye contact that reveals the soul of both. The lame man responds, expecting to receive something from Peter and John. When we came to the Lord, we were full of expectation. Our motivations, like those of the lame man, went only as far as begging alms to meet an obvious and pressing need. We could not comprehend the vastness of God or the nature of His treasury. Yet, He received us.

"Peter said, 'Silver and gold have I none; but such as I have give I thee. In the name of Jesus Christ of Nazareth rise up and walk.'" I admire Peter and John for not simply smiling sadly and saying, "Sorry we can't help you. We don't have silver or gold." They looked beyond the surface need of money for sustenance, to his need to walk and to be able to work for his bread with dignity; and they looked beyond the physical itself to a spiritual need which they had the power to satisfy. They had the name of Jesus Christ of Nazareth.

We, too, have power in this Name which is above every name in heaven and earth. The wonder is that this Name is housed in our flesh and spoken through our lips. Peter knew this yet he did not speak the Name of Jesus and hurry to the temple saying "God's word does not return fruitless." He embodied that word; and, before we come to the wonderful climax of this story, we see Peter do something very significant. He took the lame man by the right hand and lifted him up, and immediately his feet and ankle bones received strength.

Our witness is sometimes aborted because we do not extend our hand when we extend His word. In the Name of Jesus Christ of Nazareth we have the power to lift—to edify. The strengthening comes with the word *and* the service.

When the man received strength, leaping up, he stood and walked. He entered with them into the temple, walking and leaping and praising God. When we have fully received the Name of Jesus, we will not only stand on His Word or walk in His Way, but, with extravagant joy, leap and praise Him. We will have no fear for our reputation. We will not be concerned as to the whereabouts of our crutches or the crowd that carried us, but we will enter the temple with our "Peter and John." Many times, the way to become a disciple is to follow. Where? Into the temple by way of the Gate Beautiful. Jesus is that Gate, open to all. We are those who share His name, bringing the power of Pentecost to lift the lame that we might enter in together in time for prayer.

SEND ME O GOD

Send me, O God to the nations.
Send me, O God to the sea.
Let me pluck up the islands that linger
and bring them home safely to Thee.

Send me, O God to the homeless.
Send me, O God to the free.
Let me lift up the hearts that are weary
and bring them home safely to Thee.

Send me, O God to the rebel.
Send me, O God with a key.
Let me unlock the gates of his prison,
and bring him home safely to Thee.

Send me, O God to the stranger.
Send me, O God with bowed knee.
Let me uphold the days of his journey,
and bring him home safely to Thee.

FAITH IN HIS CHILDREN

Sharing the good news of the Kingdom of God with an individual is the result of divine planning. Intricately included in this plan is human cooperation. God has an amazing capacity to believe in His children and uses us in situations that require that faith.

Ananias is a good example (Acts 9:10-19). He was a disciple of the Lord at Damascus during the days when Saul of Tarsus was ravaging the church, entering house after house and dragging men and women off to prison. The latest news, if Ananias had received it, was that Saul was headed for Damascus. (Acts 8:3)

Now Ananias had a vision. We do not always require a vision before we share, but we do need to hear from God so that we can enter into His plan. The Lord called "Ananias" by name. Ananias acknowledged by saying, "Behold, here am I, Lord." Often we acknowledge our assignment in our spirit before our mind can argue with the details. Before Ananias realized the immediate implications of this encounter, his spirit realized the far-reaching ones. He had already acknowledged his name, that he was here and available and that Jesus was Lord. Only then did our Lord share the plan.

"Arise and go into the street which is called Straight, and inquire in the house of Judas for one called Saul of Tarsus…"(Acts 9:11)

It is possible that this is all that Ananias initially heard. If he heard that Saul was even at that moment praying, or that he had seen Ananias in a vision, or that Ananias was to come and lay hands on him that he might regain his sight, it was lost in the dreaded name, "Saul of Tarsus."

Ananias was honest with the Lord. "Lord, I have heard from many about this man, how much harm he did to Thy saints at Jerusalem." Ananias makes it clear to the Lord that it is not just Saul's past sins, but that even here in Damascus Saul has received authority from the chief priests to bind all who call on the Lord's name. We might have said, "Lord, isn't it an answer to prayer that Saul has become blind and helpless? What will happen if he sees again?"

The Lord's response to Ananias and his misgivings was, "Go, for he is a chosen vessel of Mine to bear My name before the gentiles and kings and the sons of Israel. For I will show him how much he must suffer for My name's sake."

Having stated his case, Ananias without further word, obeyed. He departed and entered the house and after laying his hands on him said, "Brother Saul..." Ananias believed the word of the Lord and the witness of the Holy Spirit in the laying on of hands and called Saul, "Brother." He then shared the good news of the Kingdom with Saul in the way in which Saul was prepared to receive it. The Lord had prepared Saul for a man named Ananias who would come and lay hands on him for the recovery of sight. Ananias identified with Saul, by calling him "brother." He recounted to Saul, Saul's experience with Jesus on the road which he could only have known by the Holy Spirit. He acknowledged that he had been sent to restore sight. Immediately there fell from Saul's eyes something like scales and he could see. He was filled with the Holy Spirit. He arose and was baptized; and he took food and was strengthened. He stayed with the disciples for several days, and immediately began to proclaim Jesus in the synagogues. Ananias was part of God's plan to prepare Saul for service in the Kingdom of Light.

Another example of witness is Philip (Acts 8:26-40). An angel of the Lord spoke to Philip saying, "Arise, and go toward the south unto the way that goeth down from Jerusalem to Gaza," (Acts 8:26). God asked Philip to leave the many new converts in Samaria and to go to a desert road for one pilgrim. This pilgrim, an Ethiopian, had come to Jerusalem to worship and was returning home without seeing the Kingdom. The Ethiopian who was in charge of all the queen's treasure was sitting in his chariot reading the prophet Isaiah. God was preparing him. The Spirit said to Philip, "Go up and join this chariot." When Philip ran up, he heard the Ethiopian reading Isaiah the prophet and asked, "Do you understand what you are reading?"

In sharing the Kingdom of God, timely questions open chariot doors. The Ethiopian answered, "Well, how could I unless someone guides me?", and invited Philip to come up and sit with him. Philip's question was timely. It resulted in true fellowship in which the Ethiopian and Philip, sitting together, honored the Holy Spirit and the Word. Their cooperation with God's divine plan began with a passage of scripture.

Philip did not enter the chariot and begin to give his testimony by telling how he'd gone from waiting on tables in Jerusalem to performing signs and wonders in Samaria. The Ethiopian did not begin by sharing his impressive credentials. They both began with the scripture, "He was led as a sheep to slaughter and as a lamb before its shearer is silent, so he does not open his mouth" (Isaiah 53:7). The Ethiopian begins, "Please tell me of whom does the prophet say this? Of himself or of someone else?" Philip opened his mouth, and beginning from this scripture he preached Jesus to him.

In God's plan there was a scripture that was a key to the Kingdom for this court official and perhaps for Ethiopia. Philip opened his mouth at the proper moment and turned the key. At the proper moment, God presented what was received as a sign by the Ethiopian—water, enough water to be baptized by that desert road. They went into that water together and when they came up, God snatched Philip away. The Ethiopian went on his way rejoicing and Philip found himself in Azotus (Ashdod)—two sons of a faithful Father.

PSALMS 22:9-10
(NAS)

*"Yet Thou art He who didst bring me
forth from the womb; Thou didst make me
trust when upon my mother's breasts.
Upon Thee I was cast from birth. Thou
hast been my God from my mother's womb."*

SONS FROM AFAR

Stand poised to kneel with uplifted face
before God as He comes in the light.
Stand poised to feel, to run in the race
before God as He folds up the night.
To honor these sons come from afar,
He stands poised, the wind in His hair,
With love-pierced hands He touches each scar
of those who would meet Him there.

Who are these sons, come from afar,
that blind our eyes with truth?
Lest drumbeat drown the shofar
dark legion take the booth.
Poised to hear, poised to fight
while an uncertain world demures
to hand-me-downs of winnowed might
and ill-begotten cures.

The wind blows through the myrtle
The sun stands poised in blue
While runners leap the hurtle
God's Gentile and God's Jew.

PART TWO

SHEPHERD'S CALL

"Like a shepherd He will tend His flock. In His arm He will gather the lambs, and carry them in His bosom. He will gently lead the nursing ewes."

Isaiah 40:11 (NAS)

COME!

"The Lord is my Shepherd, I shall not want." To the extent that we are convinced of the truth of these familiar words from Psalm 23, we will find the inner strength and determination to follow Jesus. Lord, with a capital "L" rules out the lesser lords of our own making, household gods breaking under the weight of our real and imagined needs.

"The Lord is my Shepherd..." When He calls, we come. Where He leads, we follow because we know that with Him we shall not want. The Lord alone is capable of being the Great Shepherd, the Good Shepherd, because He has not only eternally been the Shepherd, but eternally the Lamb of God. He knows the needs of lambs because He is the Lamb. He meets these needs because He is the True Shepherd and not a hireling.

Our Good Shepherd said, "Come!" and we followed Him to green pasture where He caused us to lie down. We were content to lie down having been filled with sweet luxuriant grasses. We ate the word and laid down. We ate abundantly and laid down. What more could there be? Who could not but envy this wholesome life? "Come!" Jesus, Our Wise Shepherd calls, "Come." Slowly, reluctantly we rise. Our faith is tested. "We shall not want." Is our security in what our Shepherd has provided in the pasture or is it in His "Come!"?

"He leadeth me beside the still waters, He restoreth my soul." How good God is! Perhaps we felt when we moved on that we should never taste another morsel of sweet grass but here it grows beside the quiet waters. How refreshing these waters, how restorative. Each drink provides inner cleansing and health. Each drink strengthens us. "Come!" The voice of Our Shepherd beckons. "I will guide you in the paths of righteousness for My name's sake." Our "good judgment" is tested. These paths are nothing more than tracks. Where do they lead? Does our security rest in knowing the future or in the faith of our Shepherd who is the Lord of our future? We move on. We shall not want.

As He skillfully guides us we gain confidence not in the narrow, less frequented path we are on but in the knowledge that Our Shepherd Himself is the Way; so that we may boldly proclaim even "though I walk through the valley of the shadow of death, I will fear no evil; for thou art with me; thy rod and thy staff, they comfort me." When Jesus says, "Come, follow Me through the valley of the shadow of death," we will respond without fear. For as the gospel writer, John, assures us, "In Him was life; and the life was the light of men. And the light shineth in darkness; and the darkness comprehended it not" (John 1:4-5). When we follow our Shepherd through this valley, we will not want—His rod and staff keeping us within the boundaries of life and light, keeping fear without.

"Come!", Our Shepherd says, "Follow me! I will prepare a table before you..." Wonderful! The words that follow don't even register. They are drowned out by mental sounds of the clattering and tinkling of plates, glasses and festive conversation. A banquet, a party, where did you say it would be held, Lord? In the Presence of my enemies! Our Faith is put to the test. Might we suggest another location? Only by denying the Lordship of our Shepherd. Jesus prepares a table before us in the presence of our enemies. Can we sit back, recline, enjoy food and fellowship without being discomforted by our enemies crouching in the background? Furthermore, are we prepared to be anointed in the presence of our enemies, to have our cup overflow in the presence of our enemies? The Lord is our Shepherd, we shall not want. We shall not want for eyes that will only see Jesus and ears that will only hear Jesus and will not hear the voice of the stranger. On this earth, our enemies will never be far away; but as we follow our Shepherd, goodness and mercy follow us; not just from time to time, but all the days of our life.

"Come!" Jesus calls at a certain corner of each life with a voice caught in cords of anticipation. "Come! Follow Me!" And He opens the door to His house where we will dwell with Him in love forever! Where we have no desire, no want except the Lord, Our Shepherd.

MORE

More than green meadows
to feed and to nourish
more than still waters
with sweet overflow.
More than the paths of
many made righteous
is the Shepherd who comes
to husband my soul.

MORE THAN GREEN MEADOWS

During a time of worship at our church summer camp, I saw by my spirit a pastoral scene. In front of me was a large, green meadow populated by healthy sheep feeding on a seemingly endless supply of luxuriant grasses. Each of the sheep was standing at a distance from the other, yet each began to be alerted. I could see their ears prick and heads tilt to an angle which confirmed the change of wind and gathering clouds. The sheep were not frightened or bewildered. They did not mill together or bolt; they were simply aware. As the winds gathered momentum and the clouds darkened I saw a few young men hurrying from the north, south, east and west. As they approached the meadow, they began to call out with a loud voice the names of the sheep. The sheep heard their names on the wind and began following the young shepherds who called them. They were led in four directions out of my vision.

I asked these questions. Why were the sheep called out of a large place where they were being supplied with abundant food? Where were they going? Why were the shepherds sent by the Great Shepherd, young? What would happen to shepherds who had faithfully fed the sheep over the years?

Here is the "part" that I see. The large tableland with much food could only supply much food. The times and seasons had changed; dangerous storms were approaching. The sheep needed more than food. They needed shelter and refuge. The young shepherds had been sent to lead the sheep safely through narrow stoney passageways bounded by caves and overhangs through a split in a rock that opened into a small canyon meadow. It took young men to lead in arduous new ways. Men who knew the voice of the Great Shepherd because He had called them to forsake everything including the pleasures of youth, shepherds who had the spirit of a lamb.

The small groupings of sheep were separated but not isolated from one another. They knew by the wind where their brothers were. They knew they were safe. They knew this would only be a temporary situation.

What happened to the shepherds who had been tending large flocks in green pastures?

Jesus showed me only one of the types of situations, that of the shepherd who had never had or taken time to become a lamb. Jesus was very compassionate towards this kind of shepherd. He tenderly told him that he did not qualify to lead the people further because he had never rested on Jesus' bosom, drinking the sweet milk of the word for his personal growth, nor been lifted onto Jesus' shoulders to be relieved of the burden of government which can only be borne on Jesus' shoulders.

This kind of shepherd was offered the opportunity to become a lamb and to qualify for a new Kingdom assignment. Many responded. Some responded with the encouragement of their flock. Some without. Some remained within their present field as this process began, others sought refuge, all submitting to brothers with the Spirit of the Lamb.

PSALMS 27:5
(NAS)

*"For in the day of trouble He will
conceal me in His tabernacle. In the
secret place of His tent He will hide me;
He will lift me up on a rock."*

SHELTERED

One of the aspects of security that human beings regard as indispensable is shelter. We often think of our needs, both physical and spiritual, in terms of food, clothing and shelter. In recent years, there has been much teaching on submission, a large portion of which has been devoted to women receiving shelter or covering from their own husbands. Those who are not married could well be envious of this God-given provision were we not assured that every man, woman and child has been overshadowed by God and surrounded by loving brothers and sisters.

While our need for shelter is universal, it is also individual and depends on our soul's climatic conditions. Because umbrellas are shelters placed within our own hands, they can be the cause of some consternation. We must never assume another person's need for an umbrella. Some only rarely admit to needing one. Perhaps it's an adolescent romanticism that like "the wind and the rain in my hair," or visions of Gene Kelly "Just walkin' in the rain." Whatever our norm, the day comes when we truly are grateful for an umbrella. If you are an umbrella holder, and not of great stature, my comfort will be measured by the degree to which you are stretched. If you do not hold the umbrella high enough, I will have practice in humility, bowing-low, and missing some of life's puddles I might not have otherwise seen. When you do hold my umbrella, let's walk close together and keep in step. Shelter is more deeply appreciated when there is little threat of an umbrella spoke in one's eye. Just when I congratulate myself on having my own umbrella, I look up and find there is someone there in need of shelter.

Umbrellas, like other shelters, not only protect us from evil but from too much good. Rain is good, sun is good, the wind is good. The elements of life contain power that we are being prepared to address. But, for now, we view them with awe from a safe place.

That safe place in a storm is hopefully more than an umbrella. In a mountain storm, a cave with a vacancy sign or some heavy brush can be useful. An abandoned shack could be a welcome sight, but nothing to compare with a well-lit cabin with smoke curling out its chimney. Even the most independent man or woman needs shelter. As I once heard a brother say, "Together, they are a shelter for their children, the husband the roof, the wife the walls." Where there is only a roof, God surrounds the children with a mother's love and where there is only walls, He becomes the cover, if the single parent does not attempt to be both.

Even as God covers us, He is pleased as we cover each other in His Name. What a blessing it is where the Body of Christ becomes a sukkah. A sukkah or tent is still constructed yearly outside the homes of observant Jews as part of the Feast of Tabernacles celebration (Sukkoth). Children gather branches from the palm, willow and goodly trees. They attach these branches to a frame, leaving spaces big enough to see the stars and let the wind blow through. These tents are a sign of man's vulnerability and the overshadowing protection of God. Meals are eaten in the tent and children beg to sleep inside its shelter and count the sons of Abraham (Genesis 15:5).

There are some days when I serve as an umbrella, some when I am a well-lit cabin, but my greatest joy is forming a sukkah with my brothers and sisters. These are days when I serve as a branch in a shelter where children can come and sense the mystery of God's presence, listen to His directions as He marks for us our path home. A cloud by day, a fire by night—God covers His children.

MOVING

*I've moved forty-five times in as many
years. But how often have I really moved? Moved
without looking back. Moved completely without a
lingering thought or nerve, or dawdling memory.
When you move, Jesus, do I passively resist your
"Come follow me," checking to see that the heat's
turned off, the door's locked, taking the key.
Jesus, help me when I move to walk in time with
you, wholly. Help me to leave behind all
unnecessary weights of provision for a future that's in your
hand. Let me welcome the foreign
land as home because of you. When we rest may my
earth be your pillow and may the rusted key of my own
way slip from my grasp and unguarded be lost
in the cool evening sand.*

PICTURE FRAMES

Change is a word without compromise. It is a word I've heard spoken and unspoken many times as I tour Scotland. I love the people of Scotland, because most of whom I have met desire a more intimate relationship with God. Most whom I have met would prefer that this take place with the least possible amount of change.

Why do many of us flinch at the prospect of change? I believe that it is, in part, due to a fear of loss. If we view change as a linear process, then we must turn our back on the past in order to see where we're going. It's difficult to reach a destination walking backwards, forever bent on where we've been. At the same time, it is repugnant to consider walking away from the expressions of God's love, whereby we have known Him and shown Him to others, in order to "continue in the Way." Initially, we know God by what He gives us. Whether it be time, friendship, affection or His abilities to create and serve, His gifts and fruit are eternal. He does not require that we discard last year's gifts or visions in order to receive the new. Because I believe in the eternal value and timeliness of the gifts of God, Father, Son Jesus and Holy Spirit, I like to think of change not as linear in this regard but panoramic.

Once, while in Scotland, I attended a conference where the speaker said, "Eight years ago, God showed us that we were to be an oasis. Now we have been given a new vision. We are to be a community of praise." It was true that new vision had been given; but, as he spoke, I did not see "oasis" being erased from the chalkboard, or as an outdated notice being removed. For even that week I had experienced, in the community to which he was referring, the refreshing and rest of an oasis.

What I did see was a framed three-dimensional picture of an oasis, the hand of God enlarging the frame. Strong, tall trees of praise gathered around the oasis "clapping their hands." Each time the frame cracked or was otherwise removed, I saw more of the picture—major figures coming and going, small details noticeable perhaps only to the Artist and those who appreciated His work. Although the oasis was the first part of the picture to become discernible, it was neither dominant nor lost to the whole. God gave us eyes with wide-angle, and telephoto lens and adjustable frames. Sometimes we need to step back to gain perspective; at other times, we need to give close scrutiny to a detail, continually allowing God to change our frame of reference. Frames are a measure of our finiteness, the boundaries that define. We are more comfortable with frames than with change. However, we are the creation of an infinite God who changes not, so we must be the ones to change. Change will come not by defining and redefining ourselves, but by identifying with God, seeing through His eyes and rejoicing in His finished work.

SEQUENCE

One of my favorite stories is of a little girl who, having expended much time and effort buttoning up her coat, discovered when she was finally finished that there was an extra button at the top. After an allowable moment of consternation, she brightened up and began a diligent search under the table and chairs exclaiming "that buttonhole has to be around here, someplace!"

Often, I confess to being caught up in buttonhole logic, totally oblivious to an uneven hem. Each button is identical, each buttonhole the same. Each button fits each hole. Why make the effort to discriminate? Why not just close the gap without measuring the consequences?

Sequence is an important principle of life. Many of the heartaches of individuals and nations could be avoided if we actively yielded to Divine Order. God knows the end from the beginning. Before we begin to search for lost buttonholes, we need to look at ourselves and see where we have, in our eagerness, jumped ahead a button or two or completely overlooked the first hole.

One night, shortly after I had received the baptism of the Holy Spirit, I heard words in my heart, "Go to Jerusalem!" They were very distinct and contained an authority that caused me to get up the next morning and take a walk, with the intention of asking someone for advice on His "Go to Jerusalem."

As I passed by a number of churches, I asked God to lead me. Soon, I came to a church called "Open Bible." I saw an adjoining house that I hoped belonged to the pastor. I knocked and the door was immediately opened by a man who was somewhat startled to see a young nun on his doorstep. He invited me in and called his wife to prepare a cup of tea. He was a pastor and he, too, had received the baptism in the Holy Spirit. As we talked, he shared with me that, at this time in my life, "Go to Jerusalem" meant to minister in my own home, the Catholic Church.

Years later, as my love for Israel grew and more so now as I keep the Feast of Tabernacles, in Jerusalem I see the unfolding of these words. Someday, soon, I will see even more clearly. In the meantime, I will always be grateful to that pastor who showed me how to match the first button with the first buttonhole. Since then, I have had other visions where, in my eagerness and joy, I overlooked God's sequence. Consequently, I have experienced some drafty winters looking less than chic to the observant bystander.

PART THREE

SAINTS AND SIN

"And, lo, thou art unto them as a very lovely song of one that hath a pleasant voice, and can play well on an instrument: for they hear thy words, but they do them not."

Ezekiel 33:32

WHY SAINTS SIN

Why do we, who have been given the power to become the Sons of God, continue to sin? I feel that often it is the result of not taking either our old nature or our new nature into account. If we refuse to admit to the old nature empowered by the law of sin within our members, we will never truly comprehend the law of Life proceeding from our inner being. The converse is likewise true. The fruit of this failure is the futility of presumption or despair.

Hope, which is not the Law of sin but the Law of Grace, rests in the Incarnation. The Word became flesh and tabernacled among us. So often, when I am faced with the temptation of sin, I see Jesus in the wilderness facing Satan, not only for us but as one of us. Jesus resisted Satan, not with the glory of His divinity but with the humility of His humanity; but not just humanity. Jesus overcame as a man upon whom the Holy Spirit rested and remained. He overcame by the Holy Spirit's power and His Father's pleasure. When we are faced with temptation to sin, we will overcome in the same manner. We will not sin when we are assured that the Holy Spirit of the Living God is uniting with us and infusing us individually and corporately with the ability to defuse death in a particular situation. He is giving us the power to live and reproduce life on every frontier. But coupled with this Holy power and inseparable from it is the voice of the Father breaking through the man-made veils: "This is my beloved Son in whom I am well pleased." This was a comfort and strength to Jesus of whom it was first spoken and uniquely spoken. But, because of Jesus, we hear the same words today and cry "Abba, Father." There is no deterrent to sin as unyielding as the Love between Father and son, and the trust that that love instills.

When I sin, it usually goes back to a point where I have silently implied, "God, I can't trust you in this situation," and have begun to formulate plan B in case God does not "come through" in time. How often this clay pot has offered advice to the Potter! I wonder if this is part of the enigma of a pot being marred in the Hands of the Perfect Potter. The marring takes place because of the misuse of man's free will, while the beauty of the finished product is a tribute to the good use of God's free will.

MARY IN THE KITCHEN

It seems as if there is often an unnecessary choosing of sides between the active and contemplative life-styles, or, as we might be more apt to say today, "the Martha's and Mary's."

When we speak of Martha and Mary in the same breath, we are usually reflecting on the one recorded instance in their lives where Martha sins in serving and Mary shines in choosing the better part. We are tempted to rally to Martha's defense and sweep at least a little resentment in Mary's direction. This is often due to our lack of understanding of Jesus' rebuke and compliment. Jesus was rebuking Martha not for preparing His meal which He was no doubt looking forward to, but for her fretful attitude with its power to curdle the cool cream of an evening set apart for friends. Jesus was not there simply to fulfill a social obligation, but to meet a need in His own life. Mary chose the better part of serving when she sat at Jesus' feet with a heart that said, "Rabonni."

One day, after a week of ministry, I was returning with a friend of mine from St. Louis. Betty had taken me to these meetings, prayed for me, and in many thoughtful ways encouraged God's ministry through me. Now we were returning to her home at 11:00 p.m. happily weary, but definitely weary. The household was asleep. The house was at rest with the touch of ordered beauty that spoke of both Betty's gifts of homemaking and of her quiet spirit.

An exception to this was her kitchen. One of her sons had been doing gourmet cooking and, subsequently, a dish-stacking feat that might have qualified him for an engineering degree. Betty looked at the dirty pots and pans. I looked at Betty and said with more than a little self-interest, "Let's go to bed; I'll help you with them in the morning." "No," she said, "I'll get it out of the way now. You just sit down and keep me company." With a feeble offer help, I sat down at the kitchen table, fighting off a small surge of guilt with a picture of Mary sitting at Jesus' feet.

As the day's activities lingered in my thoughts beyond time, they lost their place and purpose. Names and faces, words spoken and thought, ministry done and left undone, with expressions impressed or impacted, I began to second guess, to doubt. A need for reassurance began to form—that warning signal that says to me that I have been careless in guarding my mind. The warning was interrupted with almost audible words: "Martha, Martha." Jesus couldn't be addressing me, I lied to myself.

I looked at Betty standing over the sink, the dishes fairly flying through her hands as she sang joyfully, songs in an unknown tongue. Surely she was speaking mysteries unto God, comforting Him, bringing Him pleasure during the late night watch. Maybe she was joining the Holy Spirit in praying for a military prisoner in China, an orphan in Brazil. Again, I heard the words, "Martha, Martha." I looked at Mary doing the dishes and said, "Yes, Lord."

PSALMS 131:2
(NAS)

*"Surely I have composed and quieted my
soul. Like a weaned child rests
against his mother, my soul is like a
weaned child within me."*

AN ATTENTIVE SON

Many years ago, a man called Brother Lawrence took the daily tasks that were considered menial and explored their eternal potential. He made the kitchen holy and scrubbing pots and pans an act of worship. We have called his experiment "the Practice of the Presence of God." Of course, we don't really have to practice someone's presence. If you came to see me every day, I would not need to practice knowing you were there. But I would need to continually be aware of new ways to enjoy the gift of your company. If I were concerned about preparing a meal or fixing the car or watching a basketball playoff, I might ignore some greater opportunity of fellowship.

Now, you are really no problem to me because you are not with me twenty-four hours a day; and, if you were, you would also be employed in comparable tasks. But, what happens when the gracious, tender God of the universe makes Himself available to our humanity every second of every day that He has made for us. We sing with the Psalmist, "This is the day the Lord has made, we will rejoice and be glad in it;" but can we be glad in a day without being glad in its Maker?

Do we ignore God or do we ignore our work? First, we must ask what is our work if it is not the work of our heavenly Father. Secondly, how can we do His work without being one with Him and consulting His wisdom and purity? Whatever attributes are to be in the work, we will only find them in the Father and in the Son who is attentive to the Father. The work is to be wise, the work is to be pure and loving. You have often walked into homes that were physically clean for having been swept and dusted; but then, on occasion, you have stepped into a home that was physically and spiritually clean because the task was done as an act of wisdom or as an act of a pure heart, a heart of love. We can go about daily life in a whirl of well-intentioned, though often meaningless, activity; or we can make each task an occasion to fellowship with God.

If we are tying our two-year old's shoe laces or calling to our twelve-year old not to trip on his, we can be actively engaged in worshiping our Lord. Even the tiniest act is material for building a friendship.

When I was in the convent, I had three flights of stairs to climb to my dormitory bedroom. I climbed these stairs several times each day to where it could be said that I had a daily habit of climbing stairs. I also had a habit of jumping out of bed when the bell rang each weekday morning at 5:15. One of the characteristics of habits is that it frees your mind for another activity. When you do something out of habit, your mind can wander or explore or respond to something or someone else.

I decided, since I had to climb stairs, I could make it more interesting by thinking of beautiful words to describe Jesus. Many I remembered from the scripture. On stair one and two, I'd say "Jesus, you overwhelm me like a wild tiger lily," step three and four "Jesus, when the wind blows after a rain, there's a hint of your fragrance," step five "Jesus I love you," step six and seven, "Jesus, You are the Rose of Sharon. I've never seen one before. I wonder what it looks like. Maybe there's a picture in the dictionary." Now, I'm really on step ten, and another Sister comes down the stairway. I don't have to be alert to move over, because it's the custom to go up on the right-hand side. It may be the need to use a handrail that could form this habit, but it is often transformed into an act of humility or love. In choosing not to walk up the middle, we can acknowledge the importance of others and be aware that space is a gift to be shared. The Sister is younger than myself, so I continue up the stairs with a nod and smile as it is "silence time." If the Sister had been older,

I would have stopped on stair ten until she had passed, out of respect for her age. I can allow step ten to be a distraction in two ways—either by ignoring the Sister, or ignoring God's presence in the Sister, or I can recognize it as part of my fellowship with God.

The habit of jumping out of bed each weekday morning at 5:15 a.m. proved to be very valuable. To begin with, I am a person who, left on my own, prefers to slowly ease myself out of bed at 8:30 a.m. Some people consider themselves "early risers," others "night owls." They usually marry each other. I am neither. I usually feel great by 11:00 a.m. and reach my peak at 7:00 p.m. The rest of the day, I sing Amazing Grace and slowly but surely it's taking effect.

From the first morning that I heard that bell, I responded with alacrity for one reason only—I knew it was God's call. I regarded it as seriously as the boy Samuel hearing his name called. I knew that it was more than Eli's hand on the bell. One day I would jump up as an act of love, the next day as an act of obedience, then an act of joy or faith. I would decide the night before, as I had not acquired a habit of making decisions that early in the morning.

These two habits were only two of many developed over my eight years in the convent. I had not yet received the Baptism in the Holy Spirit, but my daily awareness of Jesus and appreciation of our friendship prepared me for the day when I realized that such a day as Pentecost was for all the whosoevers who would.

Some of the habits of my convent days do not fit in with my present life-style and I miss them. Some have served their purpose and have been replaced with others. Some remain as a reminder of my heritage and I am grateful.

JOHN 14:26

**"But the Counselor, the Holy Spirit,
whom the Father will send in my name,
he will teach you all things, and bring
to your remembrance all that I have
said to you."**

GOD, THE HOLY SPIRIT

I had always loved Him from a distance, this "forgotten" Person of the Triune God.

When I was in the convent, I came across a little white booklet entitled "A Novena to the Holy Spirit." It contained prayers to be said on each of nine consecutive days—prayers beseeching the presence and graces, fruits and gifts of the Holy Spirit. Month after month I would pray these prayers, longing to know Him.

Then, one day an obedient brother came and told me that I could be a participant in the Day of Pentecost. Furthermore, I could speak mysteries to God in languages unknown to me. I thanked him, left him, went to my room and found that it was true. Pentecost was not just for Mary, the disciples and some favored saints along the way; it was for all.

In the midst of the joy brought about by this personal discovery, I focused my attention on the purpose and use of the gifts, some working as tools, some as rare musical instruments. I tasted of the Spirit's fruit, mentally dissecting the superb character of the Incarnate Son into distinct attainable virtues. I ate what I could of His good while, apart from gratitude, I ignored Him. I felt little concern for His feelings, oblivious to His thoughts, His brooding love, His poignant yet pointed anger. As I became aware of what I had done, I wept—how grave a sin, our inattentiveness.

Frustrated, I wondered, "does man have to make of every good a god?" Is there no way to be faithful to the God who is the Giver of every good gift—no way to express that faithfulness in the maximum development and utilization of every good?

There is a way! It can be found in the Bible in the book of Malachi, chapter three. It can be found in the furnace. Our God is a consuming fire, Father, Son and Holy Spirit. Yet we look to the Holy Spirit in a particular way as purifying the sons of Levi and refining them as gold and silver, so they may present to the Lord offerings in righteousness.

The Holy Spirit will sanctify us if we yield to His careful process of purification, if we do not fear the fiery flames of love. If we are not refined, we are not embraceable. We would disintegrate as ashes at His feet. That which is unholy cannot come into the presence of Holy love and live. Pure gold responds to pure gold, fire to fire, almighty wind to wind. In God's mercy, the Holy Spirit's refining fire precedes the swift judgment that will come upon the adulterer, the idolater, those who rob the widow and orphan and a worker of just wages. When that judgment comes, if we have responded to Love's consuming fire, it will only find in us a cleansed temple filled with the goodness of God and the Lamb.

We are the temple of the Holy Spirit. How do we show Him love and make Him feel at home? One way I have found is to be aware that He is here and to be responsive to His desires and purposes in being here. The Holy Spirit dwells among us to tell us everything about Jesus and to enable us to worship Him as obedient sons. The Holy Spirit enjoys teaching us, strengthening and encouraging us, opening our eyes to our true identity.

One day, I was unthinkingly opening the refrigerator door to indulge in food that my body didn't need, when the Holy Spirit softly spoke through my thoughts saying, "Why don't you allow me to become your Comforter? You are choosing to have food minister to your loneliness, when I'm here and My ministry is to comfort you. Will you allow Me?" It's hard for me to understand why I would prefer a good T.V. program and a bowl of popcorn to being strengthened by the God of the Universe! However, as I repented and asked His forgiveness, I was startled by His response. He said, "Let's go make some popcorn together." We did, and enjoyed it together while watching one of my favorite T.V. shows. I can't recall the show or how much of it we watched, but I do remember that each kernel of popcorn contained so much love that I could only eat a small portion.

Sometimes we hesitate to invite the Holy Spirit to be part of our plans for fear He wouldn't enjoy them. But, more often than not, He is pleased to be involved in our small pleasures awaiting the day when we'll ask to be included in His. Ask His advice on how to spend a relaxing evening or a long awaited vacation. He's the one who inspired Jesus to welcome the children, consider the lilies and have breakfast on the beach. He was the Breath that gave voice to the Word that viewed all creation as "good!" Surely, He's a worthy companion and confidant in every arena of life.

DESCENDING LOVE

We've been told to wait,
together, in an upper room
Just when we've come to know you, Lord,
to see who you really are.
The eagerness to shout from the housetops
Amid unspoken fears and new assurances.
As the days go by, our confinement
comforts; the locked doors, secure
us within the womb of who knows
what Divine appointment.

Then one day,
The room shakes, the snakes long-hidden
shudder and flee, leaving cracks
in the walls of our mind
Walls that fall as a mighty wind
forever leaves exposed the
fanned flames of a love ascended,
a love intended to unite with
all that will wait together in an
upper room—expectantly.

BELOVED CHILDREN

If someone were to ask if I were an intercessor, I would have to pause before I answered. My hesitancy would not stem from doubt, but a need for clarification. For those who identify intercession as a life spent upon one's knees, I must admit to spending much of my life in airports where kneeling is awkward (though not impossible).

I seldom have great lengths of time alone before God and though my heart cries out for them, I find that when they do appear, I often waste them.

I remember a time shortly after I had received the baptism of the Holy Spirit when I found myself with two uninterrupted hours in which to be alone with God. No one knew where I was except my friends who had just called to say they would be two hours late for supper. As I hung up the phone I suddenly realized I had the house to myself, with its unlisted telephone number belonging to a family miles away on vacation. I checked the oven to see if the dinner would survive the change in plans and then went into the living room.

"God," I said, "here I am and here you are, and I'd like to do something to bless you." I thought to myself, "What would make God happy?" Maybe I should sing to Him. I turned the radio dial to a religious station and began singing the gospel hymn with the vocalists. I had only joined them in a couple of songs when I found myself clicking off the radio. Something was wrong. Well, perhaps God would enjoy hearing me sing in my new prayer language. I Corinthians 14:15 says that we may sing with both mind and spirit. With that, I began to sing mightily in tongues, enjoying the taste of every new and unfamiliar word. I sang at some length but became increasingly aware that God was not enjoying it as much as I was. I stopped...waited...then with a surge of inspiration picked up my bible on the table and began to read the Holy

Word. I don't remember what I read but I do remember closing the book, setting it on the table and flopping into the nearest chair, "God, I've just got an hour left. What's the matter? Am I trying too hard? Do you have any suggestions?"

It took a few minutes for me to settle down enough to hear Him. Then the thought came with the clarity and gentle strength that I've come to associate with our Lord's voice. He said, "Barbara Ann, won't you just sit still and let Me love You?" So, for the time that remained, I sat still and Father loved me.

Intercession, as well as every other facet of life, begins with allowing ourselves to be loved by God. Whether intercession lasts two minutes or two days, it takes place in the presence of a love so deep that we cannot help but identify with its burden. A true intercessory burden is one which originates in the Spirit of Jesus our Great High Priest and is shared by us to the extent that we are one with Him and each other.

Intercession is not to be grievous, nor is it to do damage to our souls or bodies. Often when I would intercede, my body would respond with what I believe to be similar to birth pangs. I would complete the intercession with a joyful spirit but an exhausted body. As I prayed about this, Jesus showed me that while this response of my emotions and body was legitimate, it was also a luxury I could not afford. He said that in the days to come I would see such sorrows that if I did not discipline my feelings and physical responses, I would not be able to carry out His assignments for which I am being trained and for which my heart longs.

When I intercede, it seems to be not so much presenting man's plight to God but manifesting God's will to man. In the stillness of His love, God reveals and lets us share an infinite particle of what the prophets call the burden (vision) of the Lord.

In this hour*, the part that I have been allowed to identify with is twofold: God's burden for His ancient people, Israel and His hatred of abortion. During the holocaust, one million five hundred thousand Jewish children were murdered. A statistic I heard recently stated that in America there are one million five hundred thousand abortions each year. One holocaust upon another with little sign of repentance. Without intercession (Not our pleading with God but pleading with man) there will be swift judgment. Even today, many hear the cries of children in their dreams.

The fruit of our national sin is already being manifested in the kidnappings and acts of perversion against little children. If we do not honor and protect life in the womb we will not be able to honor and protect it in the world.

Our own children are in most cases physically and spiritually protected through the authority of believing parents. As members of the family of God, we need to extend this covering as a canopy over the widow and orphan. We must also intercede for the children whose parents are unable at this point to stand against Satan on behalf of their young.

Chapter four of the book of Malachi (the concluding book of the Old Testament) closes with an awesome proclamation:

"Behold, I will send you Elijah the prophet before the coming of the great and dreadful day of the Lord. And he shall turn the hearts of the fathers to their children and the hearts of the children to their fathers, lest I come and smite the earth with a curse." (Verses 5 and 6)

A great many things can be said about this passage, but they would become meaningless if Elijah were to come and ask "Where are the children?"

It is tempting to conclude with that jarring question but do we hear in it the cry of the God of Elijah? Where are the children? Where are My children? Where are they running, where are they hiding? "Won't you just sit still and let me love you?" Intercession begins here.

*written 1984

I'VE CRIED BEFORE

I've cried out for help when I was wandering in the wilderness because of inattentiveness to you and capitulation to the demands of others whose cries were misdirected.

I've cried out for help when I sat in the darkness of self-centered will, malfunctioning.

I've cried out for help when I foolishly committed unknown sins, well-known sins.

But once again, God, I am going down to the sea—to a sea of black faces with fevered brows in a foreign land. I will cry "help" when I plummet to the depths of their need.

But Dear God, may I cry "help" when I rise to the crest of Your wonders and signs. May my cry be so piercing that all will see not only a willing instrument but the God who holds it.

Dear God, help me!

PART FOUR

STARRY NIGHTS

"And God said, Let there be lights in the firmament of the heaven to divide the day from the night and let them be for signs, and from seasons, and for days, and years:"

Genesis 1:14

DEAR JESUS

*You will dry my tears because
you're here where I am. You are the
lily of the valley. I thought I'd have
to make my way through unfamiliar
passageways but you are Jacob's ladder.
I need not climb tonight but rest my
head upon a stone, yielding to a starry
sky. I see your glistening eyes weeping
for Jerusalem. Jesus let me comfort you
in the soft blues of night and lilies
white, alive together in this valley.*

ALL BY STARLIGHT

It is not surprising that dreams, visions and angelic warnings occur at night. Free from the day's demands and distractions, we are able to see from a new perspective and hear the voice of God. Nowhere can this be more clearly evidenced than in the lives of our fathers, Abraham, Isaac and Jacob as recorded in the book of Genesis.

When Abram heard that his relative Lot had been captured, he divided his forces by night and brought Lot back with his family and possessions. After his return, Melchizedek, King of Salem, met him with Communion. This communion was not just a type of what would ultimately result from Abram's approaching encounter with God, but was a strengthening for it.

The word of the Lord came to Abram in a vision assuring him that his heir would come from his own body. Before he could deal with the light of this revelation, God took him outside and showed him the heavens. "Look at the stars, count them if you can. So shall your descendants be!"

Again, deep sleep and great darkness fell upon Abram as the sun was setting and God displayed the history of his sons and Abram's own end.

And again when the sun was set and it was very dark, a flaming torch passed between the pieces of Abram's sacrifice to seal the covenant which had been made.

Later in Abraham's journey, King Abimelech is saved from sinning against God. Abraham, fearful for his life, had told the king a half-truth that Sarah was his sister. But God appeared to Abimelech in a dream of the night and told the more important half, in this case, that she was also married. God saved the King, through Abraham's prayer, the wombs of his household which God had sealed on Sarah's account were healed. Sarah was cleared before all men, thoroughly vindicated, and Abraham told he could settle wherever he pleased.

Abraham, years later, advanced in age and blessed in every way, sought a bride for his promised son, Isaac. He sent his most trusted servant, who had charge of all he owned, to bring back a suitable wife chosen from among his relatives. The servant, led by an angel, succeeded in his mission.

Isaac now living in the Negev went out to meditate (take a stroll) in the field. It was toward evening. He lifted up his eyes and looked and behold—camels were coming!

He could almost see a figure look up, hesitate, dismount and cover herself with a veil.

That night Isaac brought Rebekah into his mother's tent. He took her and she became his wife. He loved her and so he was comforted after his mother's death.

Jacob has more recorded encounters with God at night than his Father and Grandfather.

After Jacob had deceived his Father Isaac and received the blessing of the firstborn and Rebekah reported how Esau consoled himself by planning to kill Jacob, plans were made for Jacob to take a trip. He was told by his parents to go and stay with his Uncle Laban and to take a wife from among his daughters. He was not to marry a daughter of Canaan.

As Jacob journeyed from Beersheba he came to a certain place and spent the night there because the sun had set. He took one of the stones and put it at his head place. Here at the spot marked by the stone he had a dream of what we call today "Jacob's ladder." It was a ladder set in earth and reaching to heaven with angels ascending and descending. Jacob lifted his eyes and there above the ladder stood the Lord. He identified himself as the God of Abraham and Isaac and made a covenant with Jacob there that night. Jacob woke up saying, "Surely this is the house of God and this is the gate of heaven." He got up in the morning, set the stone as a pillar and anointed it. He renamed the place "House of God" and promised that if God took him safely home He would be his God also and he would tithe on all that God had given.

Twenty years later Jacob left Laban, taking his wives Leah and Rachel, Laban's daughters, his eleven children, servants and flocks and headed toward home.

The angels of God met him on his way but that did not calm his fear at the thought of passing through Esau's territory. He cried out to God and that night gave some thought to selecting presents for Esau. These he sent ahead hoping to appease him. Jacob spent the night in camp but got up during the night and took his family and belongings and sent them across the ford of the Jabbok.

Jacob was left alone and a man wrestled with him until daybreak. The man, when he saw that he had not prevailed against Jacob, dislocated the socket of Jacob's thigh while he wrestled with him, then said "Let me go for the dawn is breaking." Jacob refused to let go until the man blessed him. Jacob was blessed with a new name "Israel" and the new nature that went with it. He declared that he had seen God face to face and lived.

Jacob lifted his eyes and saw Esau coming. There was no fear but the humility that comes in God's presence. Walking with a limp, Jacob stopped seven times to bow down to his brother. He gave his gifts as to God; his wisdom was no longer born of deception. He truly cared for the well-being of the herds and flocks and would not drive them. Jacob and Esau were not to journey together nor live side by side, but that night Jacob became a new man, dependent on God and at peace with his brother.

In Abraham, Isaac and Jacob we see that the night brings covenants, name changes, wrestling and weakness.

Weakness is a gift of the night. Jacob could walk a path more pleasing to God with a limp, real or remembered, than with the arrogant step of one who has not yet encountered God. In his later years Jacob was required to make a journey. God spoke to him at night by a dream in Beersheba. He said, "Don't be afraid of moving to Egypt. It is there that I will make of you a great nation. I will go with you and I will surely bring you back." Carried by his sons, surrounded by grandchildren and memories of a young man in a finely woven coat, Jacob grapples with good news. Could this missing son, the apple of his eye, be alive? His spirit revived. Joseph—a ruler in Egypt! Full storehouses! The desert sand sparkled like stars in the night.

GIDEON, BY COVER OF NIGHT

While there is a night coming when no man can work, there are many accounts of God's sons doing His work by cover of night.

God's day begins at sunset. Judah camped closest to the sunrise so that praise could welcome the night. The Passover meal was an evening communion to strengthen the Israelites for the red sea crossing at night. All night the Lord swept the sea back with a strong east wind providing dry land. At daybreak, Moses stretched out his hand at the Lord's command returning the sea to its normal state. The fleeing Egyptians were overthrown in the midst of the sea. Not one remained! In the wilderness, the daily manna crop appeared each morning as the dew evaporated. It tasted like wafers with honey.

God performed works at night on behalf of His children. At night He did those things which the people were not yet ready to see. He knows our frailty; that is why he made a cleft in the rock and a shadow for His wings.

In the days of the judges, Gideon and ten servants tore down the altar of Baal which belonged to Gideon's father and the asherah beside it. Gideon built an altar to the Lord on top of this stronghold in an orderly manner and offered a burnt offering with the wood of the asherah. Gideon did all these things by cover of night with trusted servants because he was afraid of his father's household and the men of the city. When Israel's enemies gathered against her, the Spirit of the Lord came upon Gideon and he blew the trumpet and sent messengers to gather his men. He then asked a sign of

God that could be given during the night. The outcome would give him faith that he would be used by God to deliver Israel. Gideon's fleece one night containing a bowl full of water on dry ground, another night perfectly dry on drenched ground has encouraged many to seek assurances from a patient God.

After God showed Gideon how to select three hundred men for the task of subduing the Midianites, that very night God said, "Arise, go down against the camp, for I have given it into your hands. But, if you are afraid, go down with your servant Purah and hear what they say, then your hands will be strengthened."

Gideon did go down with his servant to the edge of camp and overheard a man relating a dream to a friend which signified Israel's victory by God's hand. Gideon went back to his men after bowing to God in worship. With fear removed he could hear God's direction and proceeded to divide his men into three companies, each man having a trumpet and an empty pitcher with a torch inside. Three hundred trumpets blasting, three hundred shattered pitchers, three hundred torches encroaching on the night, "a sword for the Lord and for Gideon!"

Today, as in the days of Gideon, many battles are fought at night, and great victories greet the dawn, victories of frail men who know their God. Together we can sing with King David, "The Lord is my light and my salvation, whom shall I fear? The Lord is the defense of my life; whom shall I dread?" (Ps. 27:1)(NAS)

MATT. 23:37
(NAS)

*"O Jerusalem, Jerusalem, killing the
prophets and stoning those who are sent
to you! How often I wanted to gather
your children together, the way a hen
gathers her chicks under her wings,
and you were unwilling."*

THE NIGHT OF BETRAYAL

In the night in which He was betrayed, the sheep scattered. Jesus the shepherd was struck down. Swords and clubs waited for a sign, the salute of a student to his rabbi, the kiss of a friend. Jesus had been praying that He would be delivered from this moment of separation from His Father, this moment of righteousness become sin, this moment of utter darkness textured by rocks and olive trees and sleeping men. But when the agony was full and a living soul was drained in great drops of water and blood, a word hushed the universe "nevertheless." The union of will between Father and Son shook heaven and hell because it was a union that included flesh. It was the Word made flesh, named Jesus, conceived of the Holy Spirit, born of the Virgin Mary when Quirinius was governor of Syria during the days of his first census. This was Jesus of Nazareth who said, "Father, not my will, but Thy will be done!" History found its axis in the night of betrayal. Israel sat around the table to celebrate the Passover, while the one perfect Lamb was being sacrificed. What God did not require of Abraham and Isaac He required of Himself and His only begotten Son.

SEPARATION

His eyes were as blood and fire and love as He turned from His Son-become-sin. The moment of separation wrenching the earth as she gave up her dead.

The blood and fire and love held time in an eternal unspoken moment. Silence running deeper than the thunderstricken hearts splashed with blood, fire and love. The God-man on the cross reflecting His Father's face now turned. His Father's face now turned, full to the very eyes with His Son.

CHOICES IN THE NIGHT

In the night in which He was betrayed, Jesus made a choice. He chose to do a servants task; to wash the feet of twelve, one a betrayer. In that night He chose to bless God for the bread which He would break saying "Take, eat; this is My body." He would thank God for the cup and give it to them saying, "Drink from it all of you, for this is My blood of the covenant, which is poured out for many for forgiveness of sins."

Jesus then said that he would not drink of the fruit of the vine again until that day when He would drink it new with us in His Father's kingdom. After singing a hymn, He went out into the night.

Judas had already stepped into that night prepared to betray perhaps his only friend with a kiss of friendship. Satan, the first betrayer, had entered him. It was agreed. For thirty pieces of silver, Judas betrayed Jesus and in doing so, himself. He felt Satan's mockery distort his own lips and ran screaming into the night with a rope of remorse that forbade reconciliation; a remorse that became judge and executioner. Jesus still called him "Friend." Jesus said, "Father, forgive them for they know not what they do." But Judas was not there to hear.

Peter, thrice the chief denier, standing by a fire that same night, heard, or rather saw, in the eyes of Jesus those same words of forgiveness and in the cock crow sought repentance.

After Jesus' resurrection, on the Sea of Galilee there was a fishing boat, the Morning Star and an invitation from

shore, "Come and have breakfast." Bread broken with
pierced hands, the familiar fragrance of fish cooking on a
charcoal fire, the memory of another fire broke Peter, and in
that breaking he found strength. "Simon, son of John do you
love me more than these?" Three times the question; three
times the answer. With each "Yes, Lord" the cock crow became fainter. It remained as a tiny scar on the dawn of each
new day not to mar but to call us to solemn choices.

PART FIVE

SEASONS' BLOOM

*"The flowers have appeared in the land;
the time has arrived for pruning the vines,
and the voice of the turtledove has
been heard in our land."*

Song of Solomon 2:12 (NAS)

ROSES

Full-blown vibrant, quivering with dew, roses, I love the God who made you. Dandelions, daises, honeysuckle and lilacs in turn became "my favorites." But roses, you were almost too perfect, too highly thought of to be considered— a diamond among jewels. My own dreams and youthful abandon could not admit your cultivated presence. Still your fragrance sought me out, as now I seek you, for the lessons you have taught me, the Maker your reveal. The history of my unfolding is in the light of His beholding as I consider you.

THE BEHOLDER

Of the many analogies God uses to help us understand our relationship with Him, the one I most often ignore is that of a rose. To the extent that we come to view contemplation as the highest form of activity, we will come to appreciate the privilege of being before God. God views us from eternity, knowing the beginning from the end. He must marvel at the stages in between. He sees us as roses just budding. We are fragile, tightly folded, without openness or fragrance. He does not pluck us and put us in a gold vase on His high altar but causes us to grow together, our roots deep within the soil of human experience. Our heads bow to the rain and wind, and are lifted up by the sun. We are nourished and refreshed in order to be beheld. We unfold, not through the investigative touch of children pulling and probing, but through Divine love extended. The love of the Beholder does not bruise or tear. His acceptance and obvious delight releases deep perfume and intimate details of color and light.

In our life here on earth, some petals do fade and fall, past experiences and relationships that have served their apparent purpose. Falling to the earth, they become part of it, ultimately providing needed food and energy for the plant's growth. Nothing is wasted in God's kingdom. We need to use many analogies to even begin to imagine what we mean to God. We often associate life and, consequently, value with doing rather than being. How can I possibly please God apart from doing. Isn't activity the proof that we are alive, that we care? It is, if we understood correctly. But activity is, for many, a continued exhaling until they die. We do not see that the same energies we so admire in their outward movement are equally admirable in their inward flow.

The rose teaches us to breathe. It reveals the tremendous power of being at rest, constancy in the face of life. The Apostle Paul tells us that we know God only in part, but a day is coming when we shall see Him face to face. Then we shall know Him even as we have been known by Him (1 Cor. 13:12). One of God's chief delights is in beholding us. Are we comfortable in His presence, to both yielding and release, or do we suddenly jump up to "adjust His pillow?" Men will often run from an intimate moment to tinker with a car or trim a hedge that could wait. Looking up to God in stillness is risky. We might see Him, and then all we could do is be.

Now there was leaning on Jesus' bosom
one of his disciples, whom Jesus loved.

John 13:23

DELPHINIUM

As a five year old in Metaline Falls, Washington, living in a white frame house between the cement plant and the local high school, I had a special spot to ponder life's possibilities. It was a spot of garden. It was in fact where I stood in my saddle-oxfords to view with amazement and pride our delphinium. It was fun just to pronounce "delphinium." It was fun to point out that they weren't easy to grow on the Canadian border, but my mother had done it. She had not only begun raising the first three of six children to change the population sign of our small community, but she had raised delphinium six to seven feet tall. Neighbors would come to see these remarkable flowers.

When I looked at them I knew that you could try things that hadn't been tried before. You could attempt things that had no business succeeding, you could risk failure and find a seven foot delphinium smiling at you, and the world saying "How did *you* get here?"

FIRE AND FLOWERS

Who is this God whose
mind begets a Word
that calls forth flames
and petals.
The smoke, the fragrance
penetrate,
The ashes the faded leaf
remain.

But ashes feed the
earth where roots grow
and a flower springs
up from the Root of
Jesse, a consuming
fire with flaming
petals and fragrant
smoke, incense to
the God of fire
and flowers.

A leaf that never
withers, a reed that
cannot break. A burning
bush that hides a
voice of Glory, a word
that sears the wall
in a kings chambers
and the consciences of men.

The flowers in Gethsemane
the fire in the upper
room, inseparable, in
season, in Him.

GOD'S SEASONS

God has planted us like trees by the river, and we shall not be moved. He has planted us. He, the God of gods has planted us. No man has touched us. No man has rooted us in the earth of where we live. No man has set the Son of Love to shine or manufactured rain to swell the rivers or provide refreshment for the thirsty ground. God planted us in the midst of a world that exaggerates its life-expectancy and flaunts its own weapons of self-destruction. Yet, He has planted us in His heart where our roots are free to sink deeply into His mercy and draw nourishment from the wounds of His love.

God provides the seasons year in and year out: Spring, the time of visions and plans, dreams that are for the waking hours; Summer with its warmth, long days, short nights and green grass, even on our side of the fence; Autumn, harvest of fruit, the burst of color before death, vagrant leaves knocking on doors exhausted and out breath; Winter, closing the eyes of nature, numbing the senses, simulating yet mocking death by causing a sleep, a rest that brings restoration and another Spring. There is no reason to fear the seasons or the passing of time. Age is partly an accumulation of data that says "God cares."

We experience the seasons both as individuals and as the Body of Christ. As individuals, our seasons vary. One may be rejoicing, her life fragrant with tiny explosions of Spring, while another may be watching rich blossoms of a promised miracle fade and fall not realizing that a blossom's death means fruit for all. Sometimes we know the truth of a person's laughter or tears, but not always; if God lets us know without doubt another's seasons, we would soon think ourselves the Gardener.

When we judge by appearances, we are deceived because the seasons function at a deeper and more hidden level than the soul and perform their work without bondage to mind or emotion. Seasons continue in order and on time, following one another to form a year. They return without fail, yet never repeat themselves. One late Autumn day of having dead branches removed might be reminiscent of a similar day five years before, but it's different.

Five Winters have gone by without bitterness; five Springs with the death and resurrection of new dreams: five Summers of thinning tiny newly-formed precious fruit; five Autumns of bearing fruit, of having the Gardener taste it Himself to see if it was good enough for those He loved; five Autumns of being pulled and plucked at with those deft, tender hands until every good fruit was in His possession; five Autumns of being stripped, naked and waiting; five years of growth.

The trees have not grown because of their beauty or strength or because birds sang in their branches, but because of the Gardener. He sent the Son of His love to nourish, the Wind of His Spirit to refresh, to shake, to herald the seasons. He sent the rain of his Word to water, long deep draughts for the thirsty roots. The Gardener cares. We do not have to fear the seasons of our life because He ordained them. He uses them to make us whole. Time is a tool in the Gardener's hand, the seasons, a gift of faith.

JOHN 1:18

*"No man has seen God at any time, the
only begotten Son, who's in the bosom
of the Father, He hath declared Him."*

I ADORE YOU!

The northern lights of your hair
your lightning-filled eyes
Thunderclad Heart
I adore you!

My festive seasons erupt
at the dawn of your touch
a blush on earth's cheek
I adore you!

As bread-wine commingle
white starfall at sea
with fire-crested waves
I adore you!

I've long come from your side
born of water and blood
to stand by your side
and adore you!

Lift now my last veil
with gentle caress
as white billows unfold
I adore you!

Part Six

STILLNESS

"When Jesus therefore perceived that they would come and take him by force, to make him a king, he departed again into a mountain himself alone."

John 6:15

SOLITUDE

Solitude is the state of being solitary or alone, a seclusion, suggesting retirement from intercourse with the outside world. Though solitude's aloneness and society's loneliness are often used as near synonyms, there are some very revealing differences.

First, it must be joyfully established that we are never really completely alone. This is part of what transpired on Calvary. For one suspended moment Jesus was totally alone, separated from Father, and from the world he so loved. He bore this that we might never have to face isolation. Even in our most solitary state God is with us.

The solitude that I treasure is one that is unselfish in motive, self-chosen or at least willingly utilized as a creative, restorative grace to strengthen us for Community. Outwardly, it can be for a time or even a season though I doubt that its normally in God's best interest to embrace it for a lifetime. What is suspect in its outer form is sought after in its inward reality, a life separated from the cares of this world in the midst of this world—free enough from cares to care.

Society's loneliness isolates. Matt. 24:12 explains that because lawlessness is increased, the love of many will grow cold. Fear will cause us to imprison ourselves in our own homes. Behind barred doors and windows we will not have solitude because of the clamor of voices real and imagined demanding to be either let in or let out.

True solitude frees rather than enslaves. In solitude we learn to feel again, to think again, to believe again, to be again. Time becomes our servant and friend. God breaks into the monologue we may call prayer. Here He "calms our fears and bids our sorrows cease."

"Behold, I stand at the door and knock: If any man hear my voice, and open the door, I will come in to him, and will sup with him, and he with me." (Revelation 3:20) In solitude we not only hear the knock and let Him in but also have both time and capacity to enjoy an uninterrupted meal (according to middle-eastern standards).

BROWNBAG

Jesus,

Meet me at noon tomorrow for lunch,
I'll come alone
brownbag, expectantly.

You'll find me
sitting under our favorite tree.

Hoping no one will see us
until we've had an hour
Undisturbed.

IN SO MANY WAYS, UNSPOKEN

Jesus, you say "I love you" in so many ways unspoken, through so many words unsaid. Through grace tokens and stop signs, a ballet step, or well-worn shoes, polished for Sunday. Jesus, you say "I love you" and I see the Father looking past great mountains and crevices of human scholarship—seeking His children, and meeting them as they weep by the field lily, or the fallen sparrow.

Jesus, you say "I love you" and twisted trunks of mis-shapened visions are uprooted skillfully, leaving room for your plantings already prepared.

Jesus, you say "I love you" and I look around to find only me. Your words shaped to fit the empty chambers of my heart. I open the shutters, the curtains, the windows, the door. Here, I am. Welcome!

GOD'S VOICE

Jesus said, "My sheep hear my voice." The Bible is a unique account of God's commitment to communicate with man. Human history is but the record of man's response to this Divine overture.

We hear God speak in many ways. We hear Him in the sunset, in the child, in the summer drought. A husband hears Him in a wife's silent nod of approval, a boss's recognition of an original thought.

We hear God in an awkward moment, in an unrequested opinion; in the pain of an unfinished project, a marred vision. God speaks softly, persistently, unmistakably. He speaks because He chooses to, and He chooses to because He loves us.

One of the least understood of God's ways of communication is that of using our thoughts and imagination. We take it for granted that our enemy, the devil, can tempt us through these faculties, but are not as convinced of God's power to bless and instruct through them.

Are our thoughts our own, our mental images of our own making? I believe that they are to this extent, that we have provided the ground for their planting and can either feed them or starve them.

For example, a thought comes, "You're just a failure!" That thought did not originate from God or your new nature, but it became your thought when you agreed with it. A thought comes, "It would be nice if you took that loaf of homemade bread to your new neighbor." The thought (in this case) came from God and became yours. We can agree with Satan about God, about ourselves, about our neighbor; but we have the power to agree with God. It is in agreement with God that our will becomes free. The only confession that's worth confessing is that which agrees with God's spoken word: His current living word for the present situation. We often speak of man's free will, but we are only free when we identify with God's free will. Jesus, complete in His manhood, secure in His human nature, fulfilled enough to fulfill every man, said, "My meat is to do the will of Him who sent Me." God's spoken word today is born witness to by the written word (the Scriptures), just as Jesus' death and resurrection could be found enfolded in the Law and the Prophets on the Road to Emmaus.

Three ways of determining if God has spoken are: Does it sound like Him? Is your spirit at peace? As the word is acted upon, do confirmations follow? Then let us consider.

Does the thought or impression sound like God? Does it correspond to what we know of His nature, His character, His ways? Does it bear His fruit? Even a word of admonishment or rebuke should bear the mark of love and encouragement. If you hear the voice of a friend, a husband, or a child, you turn around with no doubt as to who is speaking, even if you're in a place filled with noise and confusion; but, if it's the voice of an acquaintance or of a stranger, you may hesitate or not hear it at all. Intimacy with, and reverence for, God will open our ears to His voice, to His comings and goings, to His silent beckoning.

Of all the ways of recognizing God's voice, the one in which I am most confident is that of an inner peace—not a peace born of emotion or logic, but the deeper contentment of the human spirit responding to its God; Creator, Redeemer, Sanctifier. The peace that is beyond the reach of the circumstances and pressures of this world and our own misguided expectations for ourselves and one another.

Scripture records a day when, as Jesus was sleeping on a cushion in the stern of a boat (Mark 4:35-38), a furious squall came up and the waves broke over the boat. Jesus' disciples said, "Teacher, don't you care if we drown?" Weary as He was, His peace was deep enough to overcome the circumstances and pressures. He rebuked the wind and released His peace to both calm the waves and his frightened followers.

This is the peace that Jesus left with us before His arrest in the garden. It cannot be taken away. This peace responds to the Heart of God the Father and is grieved with all that grieves Him. Therefore, our peace of spirit can test our thoughts.

A third way of recognizing God's word in our thoughts is to obey it. If the word is compatible with what we know of God through the Scriptures as revealed by the Holy Spirit and if we have peace in our spirit, we begin to walk in obedience. I personally do not look for confirmations before I obey or require them as a prerequisite for obedience; but I do notice that, while I'm in the process of obeying, the confirmations come.

For example, if Jesus asks me to deliver a message to a person in Atlanta within a week, I do not wait for the air fare, a phone call from the person, or a speaking engagement in the vicinity; but I do begin to get my clothes ready for packing, make reservations, pray. While I'm doing this, I may be given money to cover air fare, receive a phone call from the person saying that I've been on his mind, be invited to speak in that vicinity, or all three. But these circumstances are provision, not premise, for obedience.

Obedience and hearing God's voice are closely connected. To obey comes from a Hebrew word "shama" which means to hear attentively or intelligently. Often, when I desire to hear God in order to receive direction, the thought comes "have you obeyed what you already know?" God in His mercy, will often reveal no more than we are ready to obey in order that we be not worthy of judgment. Once we hear God's word, we have two possible responses—obedience or rebellion. We can no longer claim ignorance. The joy is that true obedience always comes by grace which has been provided us in unending supply. New revelation follows a willing obedience which, in turn, gives us new opportunities to obey. In fact, so important is this from God's perspective that He told my friend, Gordon, that there is no responsibility, only obedience, in His Kingdom. And I believe it.

When we are listening for direction from God, it is important to prepare ourselves to hear Him. One way is to search our hearts for any hindrance. One common hindrance is prejudice. Often our wrong attitude toward a person or group causes us to waver, if God chooses to use them on our behalf. Sometimes God will use a humble eighty-year old woman (who murmurs prayers throughout the sermon) to speak to the visiting evangelist. He will send a Catholic priest to minister healing to a Southern Baptist deacon and lead a Presbyterian to the altar of a Pentecostal Church. He sends black missionaries to Mexico and Vietnamese fisherman to the United States. If we were one, as Jesus and the Father are, then the above paragraph would be unintelligible as well as unnecessary.

> *I am a companion of all them*
> *that fear thee, and of them*
> *that keep thy precepts. The*
> *earth, O Lord, is full of thy*
> *mercy: teach me thy statutes.*

Ps. 119:63-64

A second way to prepare ourselves to hear Him is to be open to any answer He might give. This requires trust which is probably why most of us hear Jesus say "Trust Me" so often. If we already have *our* answer and will only acknowledge words that confirm our will, we will find ourselves deaf or deceived in that particular matter.

Before we ask a directional question we must relinquish all our own solutions. If we do not, we shall waver. For example: If I have always wanted to go to Hawaii and today I go to the mailbox and find an invitation to speak at a week-long conference, all expenses paid, with several additional days as a guest at a beach resort, I will need to pray more carefully than usual. Otherwise, if I hear a "yes," I'll think it's me and, if I hear "no," I won't believe it. If I can come to the place of genuinely wanting God's best and listening with expectation knowing that He is good, I can be happy with either "yes" or "no."

When we are considering hearing Jesus, we must remember that the Bible is a universal word. God speaks to us individually in order to apply that word to your unique moment in history and because He enjoys talking to His children. However, we must be careful not to apply His particular, private word in a universal, public manner. If Jesus tells you not to participate in a march or rally, you may not judge my boots and banners. If He permits you to collect matches and plastic water jugs for times of tribulation, I am not to chapter and verse "the lilies of the field" to you.

Because we don't really know each other, we often have difficulty determining when to be our brother's keeper and when to mind our own business. One of God's faithful spokeswomen, Iverna Tompkins, probably best describes our true feelings when she says, "It makes me so mad when you can do my don'ts!"

To hear God's voice is an unutterable privilege that we may never take for granted. It is good to meditate often and with deep gratitude on Solomon's wise benediction:

Blessed be the Lord, that hath given rest unto his people Israel, according to all that he promised: there hath not failed one word of all his good promise, which he promised by the hand of Moses his servant. The Lord our God be with us, as he was with our fathers: let him not leave us, nor forsake us: That he may incline our hearts unto him, to walk in all his ways, and to keep his commandments, and his statutes, and his judgments, which he commanded our fathers. And let these my words, wherewith I have made supplication before the Lord, be nigh unto the Lord our God day and night, that he maintain the cause of his servant, and the cause of his people Israel at all times, as the matter shall require: That all the people of the earth may know that the Lord is God and that there is none else.

I Kings 8:56-60

ALMOST

Jesus,

What did you say?
You speak so softly
Sometimes, I miss it
Almost.

Is it the "almost"
That causes you to whisper
The "almost" that draws me
close.

LOYALTY

Sometimes when I'm at a party or prayer meeting, I hear a husband or wife share a piece of information with the group that brings a response of anger or embarrassment from their spouse.

It is usually a bit of news that they should have shared with each other first or one which might better have been left in the privacy of their home.

In the same way that husbands and wives need to develop a loyalty to one another, so we need to acquire a loyalty to God. Not everything He tells us is for instant publication. God's friends, like Mary, learn to ponder even His greatest announcements in their hearts. I believe meditation precedes the timely delivery, and prevents us from exploiting our personal love experiences with God.

God loves every human being infinitely, but He loves each uniquely. We must learn to share that part of experience that we hold in common with mankind in totality or in particular groupings (such as: cultural, religious, and geographic communities).

We must learn not to share our personal, unique experiences or intimacies with God apart from His expressed approval. God desires to share as many secrets with us as His friend and bride as we are able to keep. We find ourselves the objects of the jealousy and ridicule of some of our Christian brothers and sisters when we like Joseph, Jacob's son, say too much, too soon. Corporately, as the Church on earth, we find ourselves the object of the world's envy and ridicule when we present the mysteries of the Faith in an apologetic or problematic context. The world knows in its heart that parables are not to be explained or interpreted by its own standards. The world knows enough about loyalty to wonder at a Christian who attempts to serve mammon by marketing God's mysteries.

I was in the process of speaking at a retreat center in Ohio one day when I heard God speak through my thoughts, "I don't need a water fall to back me up," He said. The mental image that accompanied His word was that of a TV evangelist reading the scriptures, using a majestic waterfall from a local park as a backdrop. The scriptures were unrelated to the theme of water; and, while any artist is happy to identify with his work, He does not appreciate it being misused or Himself exploited. If we "package" God in His own creation, we will add to her groanings. Creation longs to reveal God, not to conceal Him or become the object of worship.

God does not need props and we find none in His kingdom. This means that, if we attempt to become God's stage manager or director, we have to borrow the world's props with one hand and praise Him with the other.

It is the role of loyalty to accept God as He is and not to be continually making excuses for His behavior.

Part Seven

STONEWORK

"And you shall put the two stones on the shoulder pieces of the ephad, as stones of memorial for the sons of Israel, and Aaron shall bear their names before the Lord on his two shoulders for a memorial."

Exodus 28:12 (NAS)

ROCKS

I've always been fascinated by rock. When I was nine years old, we lived for a brief time in a new housing development in Denver. Its shoe box houses were lined up on gravel beds extending the hope of paved streets to a generation of young parents. "Green" was a color to be found only in a single-row box of crayons. Trees and shrubs and grass were still blue sketches on a futuristic time table. Our mothers sent us out each summer day to play. We came back grey. We viewed the sky and each other through the clouds of gravel dust. Not all the clouds were propagated by workmen. Some were stirred by grey Chevies returning with Rainbow bread and an occasional grey Buick belonging to a set of visiting grandparents. Life may have appeared grey to a casual observer, but not to me. Gravel was never gravel. Gravel was rock. Rock was a mystery to be opened.

"Momma, can I take a hammer outside and open the rocks?"

"Be careful!" Words as rare and wonderful as rocks. With promises not to let my younger sisters observe at too close a range or blind myself for life, the hammer was mine. Colorado gravel! It could contain anything! Silver, gold, polished South African diamonds! My rocks revealed quartz with specks of pyrite and layers of mica dazzling in the grey sun. Even the ordinary and uninteresting specimens were transformed under the outside water faucet. Short-lived glory. I remember trying to devise ways to return these to their streambed.

Rocks. I was proud of my Father, telling my friends that he was a mining engineer and geologist and knew all about "alimony." Dad, a very fervent Catholic would not have approved of my careful rendering of "antimony," a crystalline element not given to separation.

I am told that my first word was garnetiferous chloride schist. If this feat is more than family apocrypha, I am certain that it was achieved by parental patience, as I maintained a private language until I was three years old.

Rocks continued to fascinate me as I grew older. I could be entertained for as long as my ears would submit to the noisy tumbler in the basement, rocks being cleaned and polished—revealing at least one perfect agate!

During my teens, I was overly influenced by George Orwell's novel "1984," a frightening account of totalitarian takeover. Until the day I entered the convent at eighteen, I kept a small cache of Apache Tears to be used to authenticate any messages I might want to send to the underground, should Big Brother arrive ahead of schedule.

The Apache Tear was one of many types of polished stones that you could run your fingers through at a local rock shop and purchase a varying quantity for a quarter.

Today, I still enjoy looking for geodes. I have one that I found in the Texas hill country that has served as a faithful doorstop for several years. It consists of a large geode with a head-shaped appendage on one side ending in a large, protruding bill. It may have been God's rough draft of a duck bill platypus or simply a funny little stone creature that makes me want to smile but not laugh—one of the many "What is it's?" in life.

That doorstop has held open the door to my bedroom where increasingly I dream of that land of rocks where God's only begotten Son, named Jesus was born.

Before my first trip to Israel, I remember a close friend requesting not a souvenir on my return, but a rock. With great hesitation, I said I would do my best as I wondered if I could legally remove a pebble from that precious soil. How would I report it to customs? Neither my encyclopedias nor travel brochures prepared me for the rocks in Israel!

For the first time, I appreciated Jesus' words as He sat on a colt approaching the descent of the Mount of Olives. They were words directed toward some pharisees who wanted Him to rebuke His disciples who were loudly praising God for all the works of power they had seen and shouting,

> *Blessed be the King that*
> *cometh in the name of the*
> *Lord: Peace in heaven, and*
> *glory in the highest!"*

Luke 19:38

Jesus's rebuke came but it was directed toward the offended pharisees rather than his exuberant followers.

> *He answered and said unto*
> *them, 'I tell you that, if*
> *these should hold their peace,*
> *the stones would immediately*
> *cry out!'*

Luke 19:40

If it would not have remained to man's eternal shame, I would love to have heard it—millions upon millions of rocks crying, "Hosanna!"

When Jesus returns, I pray that the rocks with all creation will be allowed to join us in proclaiming Him King.

In Israel alone would be heard fissures from the depths of the Dead Sea, pebbles waking from rest in the Jordon riverbed, those singing on the shore of Galilee, a shout from Arbel. Rocks would cry out from every strata of archaeological digs, ancient synagogues and Samaritan settlements, the caves near Bethlehem, the Nazareth hills. We would hear the rocks on the stretches of beach along the Great Sea, Lazarus' and Jesus' empty tombs. The stone where Isaac's blood was spared will praise the One whose blood was shed. All blood-covered rocks will be cleansed by praise. The ones that pierced Steven and Paul, Palestinian youth and Jewish soldiers. The stones of the wells of our fathers, where we have been refreshed will acknowledge the one greater than our fathers. From Mt. Hermon to the mountains of Zion, Gerizim and Ebal, canticles of triumph will fall. Millstone and olive press, boundary lines and fortress, how Masada will sing! But for now, what God hears with attentive ear is His own heartbeat at the Western wall. Through the bleating of scattered sheep, stone hearts becoming flesh, it is the cry of Messiah, God's only begotten Son named Yeshua born in a land of rocks, Himself the Rock.

In first Corinthians, chapter ten, we find that our fathers were all under the cloud and all passed through the sea; all were baptized into Moses in the cloud and the sea; all ate the same spiritual food; and all drank the same spiritual drink, for they were drinking from a spiritual rock which followed them and the rock was Christ, the Messiah! The Messiah followed Israel for forty years in the wilderness. He offered them protection, comfort, health, food and from the Rock, drink. Yet most died in the wilderness, not knowing God's pleasure. They followed their cravings while the Rock followed them. This was for our example.

We are the Church built on the Rock, but only a part of the Church.

We are Israel but only a part and only because of unbelief, broken branches, partial blindness. "That which Israel is seeking for, it has not obtained, but those who were chosen obtained, and the rest were hardened. For God gave them a spirit of stupor, eyes to see not and ears to hear not down to this very day." They stumbled over the Rock. "I say then, they did not stumble so as to fall, did they? May it never be! But by their transgression salvation to the Gentiles to make them jealous.

Now if their transgression be riches for the world and their failure be riches for the Gentiles, how much more will their fulfillment be!" (Romans 11:7b,8,11,12)

The church was built on the Rock, Jesus. It was the same Rock that followed Israel in the wilderness, the Rock they stumbled over for our sakes. But today, both Jewish and Gentile eyes are being opened, both Jewish and Gentile ears are beginning to hear. Soon, we can pray as one to One. Sh'ma Israel.

Keep both hands free
O Israel.
Free from alliances
with kings who pursue you

Keep both hands free
O Israel.

Free to worship the God
who foreknew you
Free to respond to the Love
that would woo you.

Keep both hands free
O Israel—nation, church and me.

OUR GOD THE ROCK

Ascribe greatness to our God the Rock!
His work is perfect and all His ways are just.

"I love thee, O Lord my strength."
The Lord is my Rock
and my fortress and my deliverer,
my God in whom I take refuge.

For who is God, but the Lord?
And who is a Rock, except our God.
The God who girds me with strength
and sets the blameless in His way.

His work is perfect and all His ways are just.

Who made Israel to eat the produce of the field,
suck honey from the rock
and oil from the flinty rock.

Look to the rock from which you were hewn
and to the quarry from which you were dug.
Look to Abraham, you father,
and to Sarah who gave you birth.

O Israel,
why do you neglect the Rock who begot you,
and forget the God who gave you birth?
He, Who would feed you with the finest of the wheat
and with honey from the rock,
give you satisfaction?

His work is perfect and all His ways are just.
O Rock of Israel, today, if I hear your voice,

I will not harden My heart
as in the day of provocation in the wilderness,
but I will speak to you before their eyes,
regarding you before the sons of Israel,
proclaiming your holiness,
water coming forth in abundance.

Does the snow of Lebanon forsake
the rock of the open country,
neither will I forget you, my God
choice stone—precious cornerstone,
I come to drink and to build.
I come to ascribe greatness to my God and Rock!
Whose work is perfect
and ALL His ways just.

References for the Rock:
Deut. 32:4, Psalms 18:1-2, 2 Sam. 22:32-33, Psalms 18:31-32, Deut. 32:13, Isa. 51:1-2, Deut. 32:18, Psalms 81:16, Deut. 32:4, Heb. 3:8, Num. 20:11, Jer. 18:14, Rom. 9:33, Deut. 32:4 (NAS)

A ROCK FORMATION

Jesus, I so appreciate the way you created these rock formations, their convoluted edges reflecting light, the result of continuous pressure of rushing waters and who knows what mysterious shapings.

Jesus, I so appreciate the way you created me soft in appearance, durable under pressure, a monument to your shaping hand and rushing, living waters.

Only You know when and how I was formed. Only You know the mystery of hidden crevices and corridors where songs are birthed by the wind and the memory of waves long spent.

AWARENESS

Many analogies can be made between physical and spiritual realities. God, Who is Love, chose the incarnation to reveal the infinite value He places on finite man. God does not despise our finite senses. They are the outside of creation, the outer doors to our soul. We taste and smell, touch and observe, listen to the outer physical realities of the planet where we were placed. While we know that the extravagance of flavor and fragrance, the variety of texture and hue, the descants and spontaneous harmonies that surround us were initiated in eternity for God's pleasure, we also know that he doesn't want us to miss them! How often in the scriptures do we hear His plea: hearken, observe, taste and see. How often the heartbreaking indictment of hardened hearts; the sunset unobserved, the meadowlark's music muted by self-pity. Inattentiveness dulls the senses, Self-centeredness closes the doors to the outside. How can we be grateful when our eyes no longer see and our ears no longer hear the OTHER?

I remember as a teenager, when "milieu" was my favorite word, sitting down writing columns of experiences for each of the five senses. To touch, I said was one of my deepest delights because "things are created by being touched, possessed by being held, shared by being moved, destroyed by being thrown or overthrown." I confessed that physically I was touched while catching snowflakes on my tongue, crumbling stale bread for sparrows, stamping on seaweed bulbs and smoothing a taffeta quilt. I felt the closeness of steamy city streets, spider thread, the ripping velcro of a kitten's tongue across my hand. There were tight, tense feelings like sewing small even stitches, untying a double knot, swallowing a pill without water, removing the last strands of silk from an ear of corn, unfolding a fragile dress pattern and spreading it out on the floor. The list flowed on, touching many aspects of life and watering an orchard of budding gratitude. Today my list would be different, if I had one. What troubles me is that I don't.

I fear losing the sensitivity of our brother John who recorded for all generations "that which was from the beginning, which we have heard, which we have seen with our eyes, which we have looked upon and our hands have handled of the Word of life" (I John 1:1).

I believe that on earth there is a distinction, but not necessarily a separation, between physical and spiritual senses. I was deeply inhaling the fragrance of a rose one day, suspecting I might not have left much for others, when I became aware that that fragrance belonged to Jesus. Each flower and fruit, spice and wood is a nuance on a finite created level of the infinite fragrance of Jesus.

I believe that, when Jesus was anointed for burial shortly before His passion by a woman of holy passions, He was comforted. She, whose act is recounted to this day, broke the alabaster jar and poured perfume of pure nard over Jesus' head. As it ran down His beard to His garments and the hem of His garments, Jesus, reminded of Psalm 133, saw Aaron in priestly robes and punctuated David's cry, "Oh how good and how pleasant it is when brethren dwell together in unity." The fragrance must have remained during His agony and mingled with the drops of blood that said, "Father, that they might be one even as you and I are one."

A waste of perfume? A waste of a vessel? What a privilege it would be for it to be said of any one of us "She did what she could." Oh, that we might be so aware—aware of the spiritual significance of a physical act, aware of the needs of an Incarnate God!

Awareness is a gift. It is a habit that can be neutralized by opposing habits, or directed by divine intention toward the fulfillment of an eternal dream. At the heart of God's ʹʹʹ͡ʹ͡ʹam is man. At the heart of man's dream is God. At the heart, God's dream and man's dream are one and the same—TO LOVE THE OTHER. Awareness is a habit that clothes the heart, attracting or repelling divine and human stimuli. It is made sensitive by Faith, Hope and Love. It is made insensitive by fear, discouragement (despondency) and neglect.

As wonderful as our five physical senses are, they would be inadequate if they were not submitted to their corresponding spiritual senses. Our physical senses are used for discovery; our spiritual senses for revelation. God is Spirit and it is with our spiritual senses that we experience His presence. We have one vehicle of expression and that is our physical body that has become the temple of the Holy Spirit. When our spiritual senses respond to inner stimuli, such as the "fragrance" of the Lord, our physical senses, submitted to the spiritual, can partake and we express the experience in created terms like "roses," "spices," "mountain meadow breezes." Often our human expression of spiritual truth is dependent on the acuteness of our physical awareness. And our physical discoveries can stimulate spiritual receptiveness to God's revelation. Jesus Christ, our peace, who, breaking down the middle wall of partition, causes us to be built a habitation of God through the Spirit (see Ephesians 2). The inside and outside belonging to the other.

GOD'S FRIENDS

Jesus walked by the water on the earth He formed, and found returning the bread He had cast on the sea of glass, Andrew, Peter, James and John. "Come to my House and see," he said, the passover lamb in preparation. Sea-crystals, water sprinkled, poured, immersed in Jordon by the hand of his cousin, John, who had said, "I am not the one, but behold He comes."

Overshadowed by God, Jesus walks on the water toward the earth He has formed, the returning bread. "Come, Peter. Come to my house and see," He said.

DEUT. 33:27
(NAS)

*"The eternal God is a dwelling place,
and underneath are the everlasting
arms; and He drove out the enemy from
before you, and said, 'Destroy!' "*

FATHER

Stand by me now that the enemy surrounds me to devour my soul. Let me feel the warmth of your shadow, your right arm taut with power, your hand upraised. Halt the whispering swarms. Abate the gathering storm before the deluge. Father stand by me. I cannot see to move.

NOT FORSAKEN

There was a time when Mom was here and a time when she left unexpectedly. I think she knew long before she voiced a single symptom that she was dying. And although she spent much of her life worrying, she did her best to protect us from ever having to.

Mom lived from family gathering to family gathering with phone calls in between. Christmas was the year's highlight and the Christmas of 1980 was the star on top of the tree.

It was a painful Christmas for Mom in who knows how many ways. Plans for last minute holiday shopping were abruptly terminated by a fall down icy back porch steps. In spite of late night emergency dental work, swelling, and bruises, Mom insisted on preparing the turkey and traditional trimmings. The next day, she hung up the Christmas stockings for her six adult children. We filled up the pew at midnight Mass with Mom sitting in a front row corner where no one would see her. As the minor chords of Advent's "O Come, O Come Emmanuel" were overtaken by "Joy To The World," Mom hid her pain with her fears and made Christmas for us.

In January, I left for a much anticipated speaking tour in Germany, not realizing the significance of the strange sensations Mom had reluctantly described to her doctor and then to a neurologist before her fall. When I returned, Mom was senile and in a wheelchair.

She was a healthy and youthful fifty-nine year old with a rare brain virus called Jacob Crutzfield disease.

My father, with the help of hospice and hospital, lovingly cared for Mom the nine months that she lived.

During this time, we all let God know in our own way that we believed in miracles, and while we didn't see the great one we prayed for, there were many small ones along the way. Long after Mom's voice was gone and her brain scan flat in terms of mental activity, her spirit would rally. She would raise her eyebrows and try to nod her head when we'd read the scriptures or give her family news. One of her greatest responses to me came when I told her "Mom, I know that you wanted your last Christmas with us to be very special. It may seem as though that fall ruined everything, but that's not true. Your love made it the best Christmas of all." First disbelief, then satisfaction and a look of great peace came over her face, no longer scarred by the torment that often accompanies brain damage. As I recounted to Mom the details of Christmas, I had a mental vision of her which I interpreted according to my own hopes and expressed in this way.

The Dove marked a simple flight pattern across the
flat plain of her mind
And where He flew the wind began to blow.
Chaos as tumbleweed uprooted fled the pinioned light,
leaving a winnowed earth ready for planting.
The Dove exalting, rode the North wind and returned
upon the South
He hovered and remained with a lone Sower scattering
seed upon the wasteland that He called
"Redeemed."

In the end, the land that I had seen was not that of my Mom's restored brain cells, but of her mind putting on the mind of Christ. It was a land with no worry, a land that belonged to the God who made Christmas.

Part Eight

SONS WHO SERVE

"Of his own will begat he us with the word of truth, that we should be a kind of firstfruits of his creatures."

James 1:18

MISTAKEN IDENTITY

The prodigal leaf was nowhere to be seen.
He hid, curled up in tender shades of
spring.
The prodigal leaf unfurled in summer hues
drenched by sudden shower, shook himself.

Was he growing old in the Autumn breezes
The prodigal leaf pondered, stiffening.

Winter came and under its snow
The prodigal leaf warmed the earth
and understood.

Though He had been hidden, shaken, broken, and cold

He was not prodigal.
He was an ordinary leaf with an ordinary
life,

buried now, to nourish new generations.

FOR AL ON HIS BIRTHDAY

The heart of a man
is in the work of
his hands.

Stained glass, cut
and framed in silver
reflecting rose hues
on a desert gray.

Stained hands cut
and marked by labor
pouring amber light
on a rainspun day.

The heart of a man
is in the work of
his hands.

Not in the might
of well-laid plans
Not in his right
to "one last stands"

But in being molded
by His Maker's Hands
Being judged by the
Heart of His Father.

When I think of Al, I remember I Corinthians 4:15. "For if
you were to have countless tutors in Christ, yet you would
not have many fathers, for in Christ Jesus I became your
father through the gospel."(NAS)

SPARKLERS
(For Katie)

Dear Jesus, you know how much I like sparklers. They were the only part of the 4th of July that I could count on not to frighten me with a series of unexpected pops and booms. I knew if I held them just right they wouldn't hurt me. They sparkled and sputtered and fizzled, never lasting long enough.

Sometimes I'm tempted to be like a sparkler. To write messages in the sky at night. To be brilliant and mesmerizing. But I know if I choose this lesser good my light will not last, it will blind rather than reveal. I'll dazzle, fizzle, and sputter and end in a thin grey thread of smoke. Jesus, thank you that there is more.

LUKE 15:4-10
(NAS)

"What man of you having a hundred sheep, if he has lost one of them, does not leave the ninety-nine in the wilderness and go after the one which is lost until he finds it? And when he has found it, he lays it on his shoulders, rejoicing. And when he comes home, he calls his friends and his neighbors, saying to them, 'Rejoice with me, for I have found my sheep which was lost.' Just so, I tell you, there will be more joy in heaven over one sinner who repents than over ninety-nine righteous persons who need no repentance. Or what woman, having ten silver coins, if she loses one coin, does not light a lamp and sweep the house and seek diligently until she finds it? And when she has found it, she calls together her friends and neighbors, saying, 'Rejoice with me, for I have found the coin which I had lost.' Just so, I tell you, there is joy before the angels of God over one sinner who repents."

TWO SONS

In the scripture there is a story of a Father who has two sons (Luke 15:11).

The Father is a wealthy landowner. He is generous and treats his servants fairly. It is well known that even his hired hands have more than enough bread.

He has no need to be concerned for the future, but he is concerned for the future of his sons. He must have sensed his younger son's restlessness for when the confrontation came, the matter was already settled. The Father had released the son fully. In what is the crown of parental love he, at the proper moment, provided the opportunity for his son to choose freely and freely deal with the consequences of his choices.

"Father, I want my share now..." The Father divided his living between his two sons and from that moment both sons faced the power and problems of prosperity.

The elder son's reaction was to live in the manner in which he had grown accustomed, doggedly carrying a self-imposed burden of pleasing a Father whose ways he had never understood. Access to his inheritance unnerved him and his wealth remained untouched.

The younger son, on the other hand, lost no time. Within a few days, he gathered up everything he had and left for a far country. His hasty departure seems more the culmination of adolescent fantasies going unchecked, than a youthful adventure. The need for counsel and adequate preparation went unheeded in a "make-believe land" borne not on the faith of legitimate dreams but the fear of "missing out."

The younger son took all he had into a foreign land. He did not leave a portion of his inheritance in the safekeeping of his Father. He took everything and departed for an unknown land with unknown dangers, a land with unfamiliar culture, customs and ways. He left without a companion or servant to guide him. Each independent step took him farther from his Father, brother, kinsmen and friends. He left for a land where his Father's name was unknown, to a place where he would establish his own name and reputation. Because the land is distant, it will not be easy to return.

Scripture tells us that in this far country, the younger son wasted his substance with riotous living, or as the elder son angrily describes it "devouring their Father's living with harlots."

When one is in a foreign land, it is significantly tempting to buy security. Acceptance, respect, love are not for sale, but worldly substitutes are. And whether it was "drinks for everyone" to ensure friends for a night, or a bed, warmed by a girl without a dream, the outcome was the same. There is no true fellowship without risk of relationship and who can afford relationship in a strange land.

Like the younger brother, we often run away from the very thing that ensures freedom—commitment.

God, who loves us, allows circumstances to enter our lives that help us change our way of thinking.

At just the right moment, when the younger son had spent all, "there arose a mighty famine in that land." I believe this was in response to his Father's prayers. The famine was not in his homeland. It was in this foreign land. "He began to be in want." How many parents are able to see God's hand in the situation? We cry out for our children and then often rebuke the devil when we find them in adverse circumstances. God does not intend for them to remain there long. We may journey or even wander through the wilderness, but there is a land of our inheritance promised us by a faithful God, a God who knows us well.

This son only began to be in want when he did something about it. What he did was rather extraordinary. He made a commitment. He made it, not to a loving Father for the good of his estate but to a citizen of a foreign soil that would never belong to him or his sons.

If he had found submitting to his Father or older brother distasteful, it was honey compared to what he was now forced to swallow. His first order from his employer was to go into his fields and feed swine. Most boys when asked what they want to do when they grow up, do not respond, "feed swine," and for a Jewish boy, particularly, it was unthinkable.

It is an astonishing fact that what we initially find abhorrent, in a strange land, gradually becomes not only acceptable but desirable. Our tastes change. "He would fain have filled his belly with the husks that the swine did eat." But once again, a Father's prayers were answered! No man gave unto him: When a Father prays, the world rejects that which it recognizes is not its own. "That which is clean cannot be called unclean" (Acts 10:15). Because we are citizens of another Kingdom, the provisions and pleasures of the world withhold their satisfaction, and in God's loving providence we come to our senses and see a husk for what it is.

When the young man in our story came to himself, he said, "How many hired servants of my Father's have bread enough and to spare, and I perish with hunger!" We don't know if the younger son spoke these words to himself or other hired hands. In either case, he ceased to identify with them or this foreign land. He separated himself from them in his mind by saying, "I don't belong here!"

He then envisions a scene that is born of faith. It is totally different from his former fantasies. It is reality based on his newly discovered awareness of the Father's character. He speaks out his vision and decision.

"I will arise and go to my Father, and will say unto him, Father, I have sinned against heaven and before thee, and am no longer worthy to be called one of thy sons. Make me as one of thy hired servants."

I love this son for not making excuses! He doesn't blame the foreign citizen or those who took advantage of him. He doesn't say, " I made a mistake." He says, "I have sinned against heaven and before thee. Even in a distant land he had not left his Father's sight. In his Father's sight he had squandered his inheritance on false lovers, was unequally yoked with a citizen of another kingdom, labored in foreign fields and in the end desired the food of swine. But, his real sin, the sin that pierced his Father's heart was separating himself from his Father. The relationship could not be broken but the fellowship had been stolen. It was felt above all by the Father, but it affected the household, the servants and the land. There was an emptiness that even the elder son unconsciously felt as he went methodically about his work.

In true repentance, the younger son returns with the demeanor of a servant. When he is yet a great way off, his Father sees him and full of compassion runs and embraces him, kissing him again and again. How long had the Father been watching? Perhaps the news of the younger son's return had preceded him. Perhaps the Father's expectant hope had alerted him as it had Simeon and Anna in the temple. Hope causes us to be at the right place at the right time. Often that place has been established by prayerful waiting and tears. The Father may have stood there and searched the horizon many times but today his son appears. Restoration is not delayed. The proving took place before the embrace. Repentance began on the younger son's part when he made a decision to return. He actually took a series of directed steps called walking in repentance, strengthened by the knowledge of his Father's mercy and acknowledgment of his need for it.

When he saw his Father's outstretched arms, he was still a distance from his embrace, but what an encouragement that sight must be on the road of repentance!

Even after his Father fell on his neck in a middle-eastern expression of great emotion, the son delivered the speech that had been etched in his heart and continually rehearsed. He is not tempted by the overwhelming warmth and joy of his Father's greeting to ignore his sin or assume forgiveness. On the contrary, this deluge of love would make any explanation unbearable. "Father, make me as one of thy hired servants."

The Father's response wasn't even directed to his younger son, but to his servants. "Bring forth the best robe and put it on him; and put a ring on his hand and shoes on his feet." In front of the entire household the younger son was reinstated. The servants dressed him, put on his ring and shoes. He was to do none of this for himself.

This scene is reminiscent of one which God showed Zechariah, Zechariah 3:3-4. Zechariah saw Joshua, the high priest standing before the angel of the Lord, clothed in filthy garments. The angel spoke to those who stood before him and said, "take away the filthy garments from him." And to Joshua, he said, "Behold, I have caused thine iniquity to pass from thee and I will clothe thee with change of raiment." Joshua, that day received a "fair mitre" for his head while the younger son in Jesus' story received shoes and ring. Joshua, as high priest had been clothed with the sins of Israel, the younger son, with his own. There is redemption for a people composed of many individual sons. We have a Father who will remove our filthy garments and clothe us in white raiment.

The younger son in our story not only received the covering from his Father, but a ring. It is possible that it was a ring of authority, a ring with his Father's seal, but even if this was not the case, it certainly contained a precious stone. It certainly contained the sealing of a covenant, a commitment between Father and son.

Shoes—the younger son, very likely had not arrived with any. If he was wearing sandals, they were well worn from his wayward journey. Ephesians 6:15 speaks of having our feet shod with the preparation of the gospel of peace. God's desire is for every son to wear shoes that cause him to walk in peace and extend that peace to others. Shoes protect us from sharp stones and scorpion sting. They better equip us for our walk and as we view them with gratitude, we are less likely to stumble or stray.

Father said, "Bring the best robe!" I suspect that as well as the white garment, there was an overgarment, brilliant and festive. A party was in the making! "Bring the fatted calf, and kill it, and let us eat and be merry." Wealthy land-owners may have kept a fatted calf on hand to welcome un-expected dignitaries, but I believe this calf had been set apart in anticipation of just such a celebration. It had been waiting in a stall for a son's return. "Now faith is the sub-stance of things hoped for, the evidence of things not seen" (Hebrews 11:1).

"This son was dead, and is alive again; he was lost, and is found!" At this joyful Father's proclamation, "they began to be merry."

What an amazing grace, that sons can be dead and be brought to life; that sons can be lost and then found! One who is not a son is dead and lost, period. But the good news is that God made provision for everyone to become His sons! It is our choice, and the very reason why we are here. Now the younger son is home, safe and sound. Where is the elder son?

Now his elder son was in the field and when he came and approached the house, he heard music and dancing. It may have been the first time music and dancing had been heard since the younger son's departure. The elder son did not run into the house and ask his Father what the occasion was or even just go in to join the dancing.

He called one of the servants and asked what these things meant. Although the servant gave an accurate accounting, I believe the elder son, in hearing the news from someone other than his Father did not understand its significance. His anger over the complete unfairness of the situation caused him to remain outside. If he could have seen his Father's heart before bitterness blinded him, he might have enjoyed the party and even contributed a toast. As it was, his Father came out and found him and entreated him. Once again, a Father's love won out and years of held-in hurt gushed out. Out. His arrogance was worthy of stoning, but it cracked and released a stream of self-pity and rejection. As difficult and untimely as this breaking appeared to be, it was as much a gift to the Father as the return of his younger son.

The younger son's return and the celebration that followed had made it exquisitely clear that the Father's love was something far higher and nobler than a love that could be earned. And in fact was incapable of being earned. The elder son in frustration cried out: "Lo, these many years do I serve thee, neither transgressed at any time thy commandment and yet thou never gavest me a kid, that I might make merry with my friends." Duty keeps a record of every good work and its commensurate reward. Self-pity colored the accusation by suggesting a kid in comparison to a fatted calf. Probably, if the truth were known and if the complicating factor of competition had not reared its head, we'd find that the elder brother wasn't fond of parties. It is possible that with his misdirected attempts to please a Father, who was already pleased, there was little time for friends or frivolity.

His condemnation of his brother may have been born of envy. For we often pass the harshest judgment on that which we are most capable of. Not that he would have fallen for the world's version of a party, but we can waste our inheritance by not using it as well as by misusing it. The greatest sin of the elder brother was the same as that of the younger. He left his Father and his brother. His brother was dead to him, lost to him. He said to the Father, "As soon as this, thy son was come,..."—not, "When this my brother was come,..."

The Father, responds with a love, that he offers to each of us. "Son, thou art ever with me, and all that I have is thine!" If we, with the elder son could truly receive what God is saying, we would so deeply love Him that all rejection would crumble. We'd be able to take our Father's arm and walk into the party saying, "This is my brother who was dead and is alive again, and was lost and is found! We'd be able to realize that the same was true for us. God's vision is that both sons come alive, both be found. In the midst of friends and faithful servants the Father would grasp the younger's hand, the elder's hand and nod at the musicians. "Hineh mah tov umah na'im shevet achim gam yachad!" "Behold, how good and how pleasant it is for brothers to dwell together in unity."

TO BUILD A HOUSE
(Dedicated to Bobby Roark)

I hold a saw fitted to my right hand
called dependability
I see, I saw, I see, I saw
In steady rhythm, unbroken beat
Approvingly the master nods
His vision falling at my feet.

How can this severing build a house?
How can this division edify?
I check the measurements
The quality, the grain.

I look beyond the heap of brokenness
To where the builder deftly
Laps each board in place
Dependability, a hammer
A lightsome tool in His right hand
Well-forged without stall or stammer.

A steady rhythm, unbroken beat
A confident master at His trade
He builds His Father's house
We labor not in vain.

ONE WIDOW'S MIGHT

I have always introduced Claire as my friend or my friend and secretary. She has always been much more.

I met Claire one evening at a small home group gathered specifically to hear about a new training school in Corpus Christi, Texas. Claire was a widow headed toward seventy with many years of service in the Methodist Church. She was a veteran bridge player, a valuable member of the clerical staff during the Roosevelt Administration. She saw some of Roosevelt's speeches before he himself saw them. Claire was a "blackout" driver in Washington during World War II, shuttling top dignitaries at night without benefit of headlight.

As the meeting closed, Claire offered her services and ten dollars, the first gift to the Christian Institute, a widow's mite that would be greatly multiplied.

The Christian Institute turned out to be primarily a training school for me. A small, loyal group came to classes which were housed in a facility on the "wrong side" of town. Claire was always there. Her crippled fingers typed for me without complaint. Later, when I had a roommate move out unexpectedly and could not have met the monthly rent payment, Claire gave up her own cozy apartment and moved in with me to share the costs.

Claire has spent many nights praying for me; she has accepted the pain of my many departures; been my early morning catch-the-plane chauffeur. She is now, twelve years later, at a place where her body is having trouble keeping up with her spirit. She is facing a dependency on others that she has resisted. The day she most dreads will inevitably come, not death, but giving up the keys to her car. I want to be with her on that day, to quietly share it with her.

Perhaps, however, this is an image without substance. For, I can even more vividly picture a woman with a far greater key than a car key. Surrounded by a multitude of spiritual children and grandchildren, she is seated in her well-worn "praying chair," laughing, and telling stories—being a key herself to another generation, in need of one widow's MITE.

Part Nine

SUMMITS

"And many people shall go and say, Come ye, and let us go up to the mountain of the Lord, to the house of the God of Jacob; and he will teach us of his ways and we will walk in his paths; for out of Zion shall go forth the law, and the word of the Lord from Jerusalem."

Isaiah 2:3

TO BE A FRIEND

The world needs a friend in its twilight years. A friend that will pray. Lord, where have I been? I've not been "of" but in. But why? Have I "been in the world"for my benefit or to be a friend? Have I not been "of the world" for my benefit or to be a friend? Jesus, when you came here you were a friend. You weren't afraid of being called glutton or winebibber. You weren't undone when the locals responded to the miracle of friendship by begging you to leave the county. There, your one true friend and ex-demoniac agreed to remain behind, a sacrament and remembrance of your short-lived welcome. Jesus, for however long we have, I choose to remain.

A NEIGHBOR

The parable of the Good Samaritan is very familiar to those who have grown up in Christian churches.

A woman once told me that, as she sat in church on a Sunday morning and the pastor announced this familiar text as his sermon topic, she silently groaned, saying to herself, "What more can be learned?" She did not have to wait long, for the pastor began with verse 29 of Luke 10, "and he (the lawyer) willing to justify himself, said…" The woman heard no more, as the spirit of conviction came upon her and she recalled the many times she had been willing to justify herself. Her sincere repentance is an example of the eternal newness of the most well-worn pages of our Bible.

Who is my neighbor? "And Jesus answering said, 'A certain man went down from Jerusalem to Jericho.'" I don't know the custom of those days regarding travel through dangerous stretches of land where robbers were known to lie in wait; but I would suspect that, if you had a choice, you would ask a neighbor to accompany you. Yet, in this parable, four men begin this journey alone: a certain man, a certain priest, a certain Levite, a certain Samaritan.

The certain man was set upon by thieves who stripped him of raiment, wounded him, and departed, leaving him half dead. Have you ever felt similarly overcome? Often when we fall into the unreality of believing what is contrary to the word of God, we find that Satan, as a thief, is waiting to strip away the garments of praise. He inflicts wounds, the fiery darts that call into question God's character and ours. He departs for a season leaving us half dead, but only half. We can still hear, and how welcome are the sounds of approaching footsteps in days when our cry for help has not the strength to part our lips. The first steps continue and pass by on the other side. The second set stop and there is the momentary warmth of human presence, then receding steps crossing over to the other side. We, sooner or later (time blurs), hear the clopping of a donkey coming to a wary halt. Is it wise to hope, or are we setting ourselves up for further disillusionment?

"But a certain Samaritan, as he journeyed, came where he was; and when he saw him, he had compassion on him, and went to him, and bound up his wounds, pouring oil and wine, and set him on his own beast, and brought him to an inn, and took care of him." The certain man may not have known that a certain priest and Levite passed him by. He may not have known until later that a certain Samaritan showed him mercy. Did the priest and Levite have oil and wine and binding for wounds as the Samaritan had? If they had, it would still have been insufficient without the provision of compassion. Unlike the certain man of this story, we are often too aware of the priests and Levites in our lives who pass us by at crucial moments. They represent those whom we look up to and respect, whom we count on for help. They are often those whom we idolize and to whom we deny any expression of human frailty. There are times when I have been the priest or Levite, rushing to take care of important matters, or immobilized by inadequacy. Let us ask Jesus to bring to our minds those who have "failed us" in our time of need. These faces we see may be those of a parent, a pastor who wasn't, a fifth-grade school teacher, a coach, an older sister, a former mate. Let us decide to forgive them today. His grace is sufficient.

When we are wounded, it would be healing just to be touched by a priest or Levite; but often we'd have to be half-dead to let a Samaritan touch us. Samaritans are those who are schismatics. We have no dealings with them. They do not belong. They do not have our standards. Some even have household gods (while we unwittingly keep ours in our pockets, gods of self-righteousness and unjust weights).

We worship in the temple, they worship on the mountain. We know what we worship, for salvation is of the Jews; they do not know. Yet, Jesus said that one day none of this will matter, for true worshippers will worship the Father in spirit and in truth (John 4:23).

A certain Samaritan worshipped the Father that day; he offered what he had to a wounded stranger. He ministered when it was inconvenient. He ministered in the midst of potential danger. He ministered completely, not counting the cost. Even after they arrived at the inn, the Samaritan cared for this man and only turned him over to the inn keeper when he had to continue his journey. As he left, he gave two pence to the host and said to him, "Take care of him, and whatever more you spend, when I come again, I will repay you." The Samaritan may have had to borrow or buy a new garment, as well as more oil and wine. Today, we have a continual supply for life's journey. As we walk in the path God has chosen for each of us, we will from time to time come upon a certain man fallen, robbed, and beaten by the enemy. We will not be able to go around him and remain on our path. We will either stumble over him (be offended) or stoop down to dress his wounds, pouring in wine and oil. Our wine is the cleansing blood of Jesus; our oil, the healing, comforting ministry of the Holy Spirit, bound in Agape love. We will lift him up on our own beast (a symbol of status) and walk as a servant by his side. As we continue on our journey, our meditations will turn to One, our Lord Jesus Christ who, moved with compassion, paid the price for every man, for a certain man, for you.

JUST CAUSE

I have a difficulty with myself that surfaces every time I'm faced with a justifiable "cause." The day before I asked Jesus to baptize me with His Holy Spirit I could have participated in any number of peaceful demonstrations; "the morning after," I found I had left them behind in "one giant step" without so much as a "Mother may I." Since then, I've been continually faced with what to me is a dilemma—how do I extract righteous anger from its more petty surrogates and direct it to the fulfilling of redemptive purposes—the care of a widow, the education of a child, just wages for a workman?

How much time is to be devoted to becoming "knowledgeable" of the complexity of moral issues, school board politics, or the financing of local arts? Are we to keep balanced accounts or even records of our human expenditures? Spiritual, intellectual, emotional and physical energies are gifts of God. How shall we use them?

For example, a brother recently showed concern that I might be in spiritual danger because of my love for Israel. He rightly saw the danger in my directing my attention toward a land and a people rather than toward God. As I considered our conversation, my mind went back to the days when I would not eat grapes because the teeth of migrant farm workers were set on edge. Their unions often made in the flesh, could not become Communion bread. Instead, political machines were activated that worship mammon and soon devour the people they would save. A horizontal approach to injustice leads to a crusading spirit that can blind us to the totality of truth and harden our hearts toward those who cannot see our portion of truth as being the whole, or at least, the most important in priority.

I love the Jewish nation and the Jewish people. Because I do, I need to direct my heart toward God and think, feel and speak His thoughts toward His ancient people whom He has never forsaken. I must speak, not on behalf of Israel, but on behalf of Israel's God. I enter the political arena with the Advocate's power; I come to the world's party dressed in garments of praise. In the world but not of it, we can feed the hungry and clothe the naked.

"Pure religion and undefiled before God and the Father is this, to visit the fatherless and widows in their affliction, and to keep oneself unspotted from the world."

James 1:27

ISAIAH 66:12-13
(NAS)

For thus says the Lord, "Behold, I extend peace to her like a river, and the glory of the nations like a overflowing stream; and you shall be nursed, you shall be carried on the hip and dandled upon her knees. As one whom his mother comforts, so I will comfort you; and you will be comforted in Jerusalem."

JERUSALEM AT A DISTANCE

I loved Jerusalem; She is ever in my thoughts, yet because I loved her I only came to her on my Father's business. It was at a distance that I could see her clearly—by the shores of Galilee I remembered her in the movement of the waters, the wind-swept trees, the children's laughter. It was in the wilderness I fought for her, outside the walls I bought her. In the friendship of Bethany, I was at home with her; from a hill I looked down upon her with weeping.

Do not be afraid to step back. You cannot leave Jerusalem. She is in your heart as you are in Mine.

TWICE ANOINTED

Jesus' feet twice anointed
stand and firm the quaking heights.
Planted on the Mount of Olives
Waiting for the Feast of lights.

Jesus' feet twice anointed
Once for heaven, once for earth
Treading out the wine of vengeance
in His mercy giving birth.

Jesus' feet twice anointed
tracing steps for men to see
Pierced and wounded, bleeding glory
Mark the path of victory.

BEAUTIFUL ON THE MOUNTAINS

"How beautiful upon the mountains are the feet of him that brings good news..." (Isaiah 52:7)

Good news is the announcement of peace, happiness and salvation. It is the announcement to Zion that Her God reigns. If God did not reign there would be no possibility of Good News. Apart from God's reign there is no peace, no happiness, no salvation. But our God does reign. He reigns not from afar but as Immanuel, God-with-us. He dwells between our shoulders. He resides in our hearts. He works through our hands. He speaks with our voice. He rules without coercion. He moves with love. Can The Head say to the feet, "I have no need of you?" Jesus often chooses to reveal Himself through His body. He identifies with us. When Paul (Saul of the tribe of Benjamin) sought to apprehend and imprison Jesus' followers, he was himself apprehended and became a prisoner of Jesus Christ.

A brilliant light, a question in the Hebrew tongue intercepted Paul with a revelation he would never forget: "I am Jesus whom thou persecutest." (Acts 9)

There are few spokesmen as persuasive as Paul in testifying to this truth, that when we persecute our brothers and sisters we are persecuting Jesus. "Whatsoever you do to the least of my brothers, that you do unto me." (Matt. 25:40)

Paul testified not only by ceasing in his persecution, but by serving Jesus in His body. In Acts chapter 28 we see that Paul was no respecter of persons. He gathered a bundle of sticks to throw on a fire kindled by kind barbarians who were aware of the effects of the rain and cold on the shipwrecked survivors. Secure between God's shoulders, Paul shook off the viper that fastened on his hand. It fell into the flames that had been fed by Paul's service. Paul did not receive the venom because of love for the least. It was through that love that the chief's father received healing as well as others on the island.

Today, we must once again face the question "lovest thou, me?" We may not all be called as Peter the Apostle to be an overseer of the flock but we must all be willing to feed the lambs and sheep in Christ's Body. (John 21) We are privileged to break the bread of encouragement, to feed each other with the sincere milk of The Word. (I Peter 2:2) We are called to love one another, to forgive, to heal. By the shedding of the precious blood of Jesus, the spotless lamb, we have been reunited with God.

When we consider the inheritance of Benjamin we may see Jesus gently lifting a wobbly lamb, His strong hands positioning it securely across His shoulders. This is a tender scene, one which we may often have experienced during the days of our searchings, our wanderings and our entanglements. But there is also a vision in God's heart of a people who will rest against His heart, dwelling face to face— nourished, comforted. God desires a relationship where we not only view life looking over His shoulder as one being carried, but where we walk by His side. "Who is this coming up out of the wilderness, leaning on the arm of her beloved," questions Solomon. (Song of Solomon 8:5)

Benjamin's inheritance is intact, extending to all who will come, an invitation to the Bride of Christ, a gift from the Father to the Son.

Beloved of the Lord, may you dwell in security by Him who shields you all the day—may YOU dwell BETWEEN HIS SHOULDERS.

Books can be ordered from:

Accord Company
P.O. Box 326
Kingsland, TX 78639

or

Companion Press
P.O. Box 351
Shippensburg, PA 17257